IS IT JUST ME OR IS IT *still* KAK?

2 KAK 2 FURIOUS

Published by Two Dogs
an imprint of SchreiberFord Publications

•

SchreiberFord Publications
PO Box 50664, The Waterfront, Cape Town, 8001

info@twodogs.co.za
www.twodogs.co.za

•

First published 2008
Reprinted 2009
3 5 7 9 8 6 4 2

•

Publication © 2008 Two Dogs
Text © 2008 Tim Richman, Grant Schreiber

•

•

Publishing director: Daniel Ford
Managing director: Grant Schreiber
Publishing manager: Tim Richman
Art director: Francois Pretorius
Proof reader: Ania Rokita

•

Distributed by Quartet Sales & Marketing

Printed and bound by Paarl Print, Oosterland Street, Paarl, South Africa

•

ISBN 978 1 92013 726 7

Mush, huskies! Mush!

About the authors

Tim Richman and Grant Schreiber are the authors of *Is It Just Me Or Is Everything Kak?* They are also the people behind Two Dogs books.

Acknowledgments

Thanks (and angelic praises) to Julie Rowand and Rupert Butler.

Thanks also to everyone who contributed ideas for the book and offered feedback, including Francois Pretorius, Ania Rokita, Kerry Rogers, Mandy J Watson, Erika Bornman, Brian Richman, Bob Rowand, Leigh Herringer, Mike Dixon, Greg Boyes, James Price, James Carolin, Jon Roberts, Tudor Caradoc-Davies, Margie Gie, Warren Barkhuizen, Andrew Eaton, Warren Kirsten, Toni Lee Stephan, the *Tos* guys and the Makgokolo crew: Larry & Lyns, Gabriel & Callia, Brad & Harriet and James.

Special mention to Tricia Rowand and Michelle Erasmus and, again, to the SASASU men – who see a lot of the kakness out there and call it like it is.

To the angle-grinding son of a bitch next door.

Introduction

You probably predicted this. If you read our first book, *Is It Just Me Or Is Everything Kak?*, you probably figured there would be a shameless attempt to cash in on its commercial success somewhere down the line. And, of course, you figured right. Just because we loathe those soulless, rapacious, money-grubbing capitalist dogs out there, doesn't mean we can't fight for the scraps. The best you could have hoped for was an inspired, *Godfather II*-reminiscent, original-trumping follow-up – disguising a shameless attempt to cash in on the commercial success of the first book. At this point, we would like to refer you to the entry on **Sequels**, and remind you that the original book is still on sale in all good book stores and online.

In the meantime, please take note of the following:

1) We apologise for the excessive cross-referencing. Turns out the kakness of the world is interconnected on so very many levels, and we wouldn't want you thinking we'd forgotten what we said elsewhere. *Kak 1* obviously refers to said original book. If you haven't read it yet, it is still on sale in all good... you know.

2) A lot of really bad things start with the letter S. "Shit", for example. There's just no way around it. This is why S is so long. Conversely, not much starts with the letter Z. Which at least gives us a reason to be grateful for the word "Zuma".

Blistering regards.

A

Affirmative Action in tertiary education

Starting with affirmative action again, are we? Yup. Not like it's getting any better. And, as you may have noticed, we are shameless; we'll do anything to grab your attention. (Turn the page for pictures of naked women wrestling in chocolate sauce! Maybe...)

Even teenagers – that is, South Africans who were not yet born when Nelson Mandela was freed, many of whom have been in mixed classes since pre-primary school – are subject to affirmative action on application to university these days. Nowadays, a white applicant to the University of Cape Town medical school, for example, reportedly requires a 91 per cent matric aggregate, whereas a black applicant only requires...

You know what? I'm over it. Can't be bothered. Refuse to get steamed up by affirmative action any more. Just an unnecessary waste of energy. Who cares anyway? It only affects the government, the economy, service delivery, education, entertainment and the entire population. A minor irritant. An annoyance. A flea bite on the bottom.

Now, Afrikaans music on the other hand – holy moly, that's a bagful of mouth ulcers right there...

Afrikaans music

Sometimes, in my darker moments, when I consider the extraordinary popularity of Afrikaans music, I just can't go on. The world is indeed a vexatious place that it lets bonehead beats rule the South African music market as they do.

I'm not talking about boeremusiek here. You know, okes on accordions singing liedjies and having a jol. They're fine. Well no, they're not fine. They're horrendous actually and choosing between listening to them or listening to a Celine Dion/Barbra Streisand duet* would be like choosing which arm you'd like sawn off. But because you never hear them unless you physically venture out beyond the Boerie Curtain, they're not much of a bother. Unlike Afrikaans music, which is HUGE! And it FINDS YOU! At the rugby, in shopping malls, during commercial breaks…

Someone please enlighten me as to how albums such as *Bakgat Sokkie Top 20* and the annual *Bokjol Somerpartie* abomination can afford so much prime-time advertising space. And why Steve Hofmeyr is such a god in this country. And how Bok van Blerk can fill Loftus Versveld to the brim with demented fans by singing about a Boer general with a rhyme-able name. And how the gelled-hair, open-shirt, kak-music, cheeseball-male-singer formula works. Van Blerk, Kurt Darren, Nicholis Louw, Jaco, Robbie Wessels, Robbie Klay – are these guys the same person in disguise? Or are they Steve Hofmeyr's illegitimate kids, genetically modified by Wouter Basson to send out subliminal messages that hypnotise unsuspecting young Afrikaners?

Probably Wouter's fault. *Daai kabouter.*

---

* Which exists, by the way. It's called *Tell Him*. The Americans use it as part of their torture repertoire at Guantanamo Bay. I imagine.

Airport advertising

Just to make the flying process that much more painful they replay the same ad on two-minute loops in the departure hall so that you can't sit in one place for longer than ten minutes without wanting to stab someone with a rusty spoon. Screw you, Investec! Then, just when you think the agony of flying is over, they do it again at the baggage carousel as you're waiting to see if your case has been rifled through by your thoughtful baggage handler. Screw you, Daikin air conditioners!

"All credit to them"

The stock phrase at the post-match interview. What, you don't want to take *some* credit? Maybe just a little bit? A smidgen? How about credit for the phrase "all credit to them"? Remember, it's a team effort. It's about stepping up to the plate. It's about respecting the opposition.

And now over to the panel of ex-players who will dispense their own cliché-jukebox wisdom and insight… At the end of the day, it's what happens on the field that counts.* It's about bringing your A-game. It's about giving 110 per cent for the full 80 minutes… Of course, this percentage changes according to who's talking. Certain experts deem 110 per cent a slacker's effort and demand up to 300 per cent for the full 80 minutes. No half measures here. Why it isn't 300 per cent for the full 240 minutes, I don't know. It's equally moronic. Morons. (See **Morons**.)

Do you think these guys talk like this the rest of the time too? Can you imagine Warren Brosnihan and Owen Nkumane cooking breakfast together?

> Warren Brosnihan: Who's hungry for it? Who's hungry for it?
>
> Owen Nkumane: Good to go! Breakfast time!
>
> Warren Brosnihan: We should get Jean de Villiers to cook us some eggs. He is the ultimate poacher.
>
> Owen Nkumane: I'll give it a try – try time!
>
> Warren Brosnihan: Looks like you needed no introduction to that try line.

OWEN NKUMANE: It's about passion.

WARREN BROSNIHAN: It's about pride.

OWEN NKUMANE: Off-load the salt, bru.

WARREN BROSNIHAN: You cook with sumptuous speed.

OWEN NKUMANE: That's some telling salt.

WARREN BROSNIHAN: Game, set and match.

* Translated from "At da end of da day, it's what happens on da field dat counts."
Thanks, Naas.

The arms deal

Let's, for argument's sake, just assume that the entire government was bribed at some stage during the arms-deal negotiations. Every other government in the world does it, there's nothing unique or particularly surprising about it, so why should ours be any different? *C'est la vie*. Or whatever *c'est la vie* is in German. As depressing a thought as that may be, even more depressing – and downright embarrassing, really – is the realisation that our newly enriched fat cats in power got the wrong stuff. The useless tossers.

If every politician who had anything to do with the arms deal had just received a million rand from South African taxpayers, then stepped aside to let someone who knew what he was talking about actually choose the kit we needed, we'd all be cool with it today. Probably wouldn't have gone down so well at the time admittedly, but just look what they've given us: frigates, submarines and fighter jets that we can't afford to run or crew and which are almost entirely useless given the fact that neither Swaziland nor Namibia look likely to invade any time soon.* Let's take a quick look:

• Our four Meko-class frigates, which the government likes to call corvettes so they sound smaller and less of a waste of money but are actually frigates, are built with stealth characteristics to reduce their radar signatures. This is important when you are being attacked by other warships. But not when being attacked by other warships is never going to happen. (Or when you live in a shack in Soweto without a running water supply.) The frigates came in at more than a billion rand each, with a further R8 million a day required to operate them. Which is why we can only run two of them at a time and can't protect our coastline. (The navy has now declared a desperate need for eight to 12 multipurpose patrol boats, at R250 million to R300 million a pop, to do this.)

• Our three Type 209 diesel-electric attack submarines, coming in at about R1.5 billion a piece, are probably more pointless. Even if we could crew and operate all of them – or just one of them, which seems to be a struggle – they would have no use. Not unless we take to torpedoing illegal Patagonian toothfish trawlers.

• Then we have our advanced fourth-generation JAS 39 Gripen fighters. These would sort of make sense if we were still fighting the Angolan bush war. Or if the pilots of the Zimbabwean air force suddenly went renegade and bombed Pretoria in their 1970s-era MiGs. Ironically we could have been attacked by crop-dusters in mid-2008 and we wouldn't have been able to defend ourselves, as our Cheetah squadron had to be decommissioned four years earlier than expected due to budget constraints. As of September 2008 the air force had received four Gripens – and insufficient funds to operate them and our new Hawk trainers for the year ahead.

People who know about SA's defence requirements have called the purchase of our new non-operational naval armada and under-funded air force the equivalent of having a luxury car without being able to afford petrol or servicing fees when all that was needed was a general-utility mountain bike. But that's not entirely accurate: it's more like buying the *Starship Enterprise* when what we needed was an orange squeezer.

Sigh.

After all that, here's some food for thought: the arms deal was worth R30 billion when it was signed in 1999, but in the next five years the government will likely be signing contracts for power stations to the value of R600 billion. We can safely assume that a good portion of that money will go towards funding politicians' election campaigns and Mercedes-Benzes, but let's just hope Cabinet orders the right things this time round. And that we don't end up with power stations run by homeless people pumping hand-crank dynamos.

* And besides, a million bucks each was cheap at the price. British and German investigators suspect that the bribes ultimately totalled over R1 billion. Yasis!

Attention-seeking faux-lesbian kissing

It's a tragic day when you admit you're over lesbianism. But I am. The forbidden mystery of it all has just disappeared in an avalanche of overexposure and commercial exploitation. That Britney and Madonna publicity stunt was probably the start of it, but did you see the *Grey's Anatomy* episode when the two big chicks kissed? Lame, if you ask me. Like *Grey's Anatomy* in general. And Britney. And Madonna. (See **Grey's Anatomy**.)

Austrians

Austrians. What's their vibe? Are they all clinically deranged? If media reports are anything to by, this seems to be the only sensible conclusion.

First there was the guy who kidnapped the 12-year-old girl and kept her in a basement for six years. Then there was the guy who kidnapped his own daughter, kept her in the basement – this time for 24 years – and fathered seven children with her. And then there was the guy who axed to death his wife, child, parents and father-in-law – because he wanted to spare them the shame of finding out that he had blown all their money. (Thoughtful!)

Maybe it's a role-model issue. Think about it. How many famous Austrians are there? Two. Hitler and Arnie. One, the exterminator of the Jews; the other, a terminator sent back through time to bring about the destruction of the human race. No wonder these people are confused.

B

Bafana Bafana

Where do you suppose all the money we're paying for Joel Santana to coach our national soccer team is going? He's reportedly on anything between R1 million and R1.5 million a month, contracted until the end of the 2010 World Cup – so what's he doing with it all? Swimming in it? Collecting Bugatti Veyrons? Saving up to buy himself a small country?

I wouldn't mind his job for that salary, got to say. Hell, I'd take it at R995K and still be happy. Come on, SAFA, it's a bargain! And it's not like it would make a difference either way. With all the infighting, pocket lining and inept management that seems to define the local soccer scene, they could put Alex Ferguson in charge or they could let the Coco Pops monkey have a go and there would be virtually no discernible rise or drop in form.

BBC, CNN, Sky and international news in general

Local news is bad enough as it is; it's just plain absurd what goes on in this country, and it's so compelling (and outraging) because everything relates back to you. But what about international news? Turn on BBC, CNN, Sky or, if you're a little more open-minded (and a member of the Axis Of Evil), Al Jazeera, and it's just mayhem out there. Incomprehensible mayhem. Hurricane here, earthquake there, bomb blast over there… And the one that affects you the most, because you can see his bloodied face and imagine his pain, is the poor villager in Zimbabwe who was tortured by Zanu-PF goons. The estimated 200,000 deaths in Burma or 80,000 casualties in China or the thousands dead in Iraq just defy comprehension. No wonder Sky focuses three-quarters of its budget on reporting royal scandals and missing children.

Best-dressed lists

Guys, this is what you need to know: best-dressed lists are stupid and Kate Beckinsale is hot. You can skip to the next one now. Girls, here goes.

Right, so here we have *Marie Claire*, August 2008. Behold, the 101 best-dressed celebrities of the year.

At 101, setting the tone in a dress that has quite possibly had several of her Chihuahuas ironed into it, the all-conquering princess of nouveau trash herself, Paris Hilton.

In at 92 – obviously been at the pies again – is Fergie from the Black Eyed Peas, looking vaguely psychotic, as though she's contemplating her revenge on the guy who's just grafittied her blouse. Because that's obviously what's happened.

Trumping Paris at 89 is sister Nicky Hilton. Not only a stupider outfit, but dumber-looking too. Evidently it's possible.

At 82, Salma Hayek wears a floor-length emerald gown that screams dire, then at 69, 68 and 66, it is respectively Doutzen Kroes as a sack, Nicole Richie as an airhead and one of the Olsen twins as a bag lady – before Gisele Bündchen outdoes them all with her German-lesbian-biker vibe at 65. Yikes.

Moving into the 50s, Keira Knightley struts her ano-Auschwitz impression, Lucy Liu has had a leprechaun vomit on her overcoat and Daphne Guinness (meh? Me neither) has quite clearly lost a bet. Bear with me.

The 30s are truly special, with Maggie Gyllenhaal's clown number losing out to Olsen number two's dwarf-appearance-inducing breast-level waistline, which in turn loses out to a Lindsay Lohan slut-tacular, while Lily Allen beats them all with a dress to make young children cry – until you turn the page and see Kate Hudson in a shimmery green outfit, evidently a flying suit of sorts, with kotch marks near the top. Jesus wept.

At 26 we have Jennifer Lopez looking quite frankly enormous in a fitted tent of some sort, probably designer, then it's Victoria Beckham wearing a colourful hanky and that same gormless expression at 19, with the ever-so-annoying Sarah Jessica Parker wearing who really cares at 17.

The pain is really kicking in now, but we'll get through it, don't worry, with Sofia Coppola in a nightgown at 14, Rihanna as par-for-the-course fashion victim at 12 and Katie Holmes as the shimmering-red bride of Satan – which is appropriate, I suppose (see **Tom Cruise**) – at 5.

And finally, we've made it to number one, to one Agyness Deyn who, if you don't know already, is *the* shit in the fashion industry at the moment. She is so hot right now it's just ridiculous. Has there ever been a model with so many looks? Which is to say that one day she'll let her cat dress her, and the next it's the budgie's turn. Then she'll actually wear the cat and the budgie, in combination with a hat she found in a dumpster and really silly shoes.

Silly. Kinda says it all.

I have a better suggestion. Take Kate Beckinsale – 98, travesty! – and just repeat her for 24 pages. And add Daria Werbowy (71) and Natalie Portman (20) if there's still space. That goes for all best-dressed lists.

P.S. This is genuinely sound advice. It will make the world a better place.

Biz-speak

This is one of those topics that everyone in the world takes the piss out of, a bit like Uncle Bob's Hitler tache. We all shake our heads in dismay at the thought of business speak, so you'd think that, going forward, we might take the bull by the horns, hit the ground running, push the envelope and just give up on the hackneyed phrases with no meaning or sincerity… But then you still get this: "South-South exchanges are hugely powerful and companies that are looking at business opportunities and social-investment opportunities have a real opportunity to facilitate collaboration and sharing of best practice and can help prevent the reinventing of wheels and duplication of effort and finances."

This is not made up. It is a real quote written by a real person, who publicly represents a real international charity that I'll have the decency not to name. She is attempting to communicate with real humans. Does she not realise how much potential largesse she is throwing away with comments like this? Because if I were a multibillionaire playboy philanthropist about to donate millions to her charity, I'd recoil in horror when I read this, and give it all to Errol the bergie who sleeps in a hedge down the road. Luckily for her I'm not a multibillionaire playboy philanthropist. Not so lucky for Errol.

Black cars

Too many of them.

Blame culture

These are the standard default positions of South Africans today:
1. Black people blame apartheid – that is, white people – for everything they don't like.
2. White people blame government – that is, black people – for everything they don't like.
3. Coloured and Indian people blame apartheid *and* government – that is, black people *and* white people – for everything they

don't like.

While the injustices of the apartheid regime should rightly never be dismissed, it is surely time to accept that some responsibility for the state of things today lies with the leaders of today – and that not all of it is the fault of people who were last in power 15 years ago. Equally, while the current government is undoubtedly mired in a heady blend of corruption, nepotism, incompetence and negligence, there is little point in just throwing your hands in the air and pointing fingers whenever something doesn't go your way. So let's all channel some nice positive vibes, work together on this one a bit and, you know, try to make the world a better place. Maybe if we all do a little bit here and there, the apartheid legacy will wash out at some stage, and the current lot in charge will take the hint.

As anti-apartheid activist and Rivonia treason trialist Denis Goldberg said in a recent lecture, "Stop blaming everyone else – be the power and the glory."

Amen, brother.

James Blunt

If you didn't know already, James Blunt has become Cockney rhyming slang for an intimate part of the female anatomy. Appropriate, no?

Booing rugby fans

There are the rugby "fans" who shout at the kicker as he's lining up to take a shot at goal. And there are the ones who use the phrases "Ref, you're missing a good game, ref!" and "Where's your guide dog, ref?" *every single game.* And there are the ones – born and bred in Cape Town – who go to Newlands to support the All Blacks. (Go live in Rotorua, why don't you?) And don't forget the fair-weather Durban and Pretoria crowds who see fit to boo the Boks when they lose.

James Blunts, the lot of them.

Brain Box

Barking mad. Both the show and anyone who calls in at R7.50 a minute thinking they're going to win anything. And yet it's strangely compelling...

Don't know what I'm on about? Check out e.tv, late at night.* An attractive presenter in a suitably revealing outfit takes calls from viewers – who are presumably not very smart or rather trolleyed, or both – trying to answer the on-screen riddle as frenetic music plays and alarm bells ring, both literally and figuratively. For the first half hour you'll be speechless, trying to work out a) how people can fall for something like this, b) how a bra can manufacture that much cleavage and c) what the hell the answer is. But don't try working it out. It's waaaay random. Oh, 973, is it? And how did you come up with that? The fairies tell you? You just magic it out your rear? May as well have.

The technical term for this kind of show is apparently "participation television". I'd think "gambling television" is a bit closer to the mark but hey, I'm no media specialist. Amazingly, it's legal. And it should stay that way – as a dreadful warning to those of us gaping on in wonderment that television viewers are, in the main, not brain boxes.

*It's more entertaining than the soft porn, and the lighting's a whole lot better.

Bring-your-meal dinner parties

You know what? It's my night off when you invite me over so I really don't feel like bringing a salad. Or dessert. You get a bottle of wine and maybe some flowers if you're a pretty girl, but that's it, okay?

C

Carte Blanche's time slot
MNET needs to move this show to Tuesdays or something. I've got Sunday losers as it is and it's really getting me down.

Cashiers
Smile, please!

Ccing on work emails
Either it's an arse-covering manoeuvre – look everyone, I'm doing my job! – or it's an appeal to colleagues to get something done. But because it doesn't apply to me (or 27 of the other 29 people on the mailing list, for that matter), I am now irritated with you for wasting my time and clogging up my inbox. So when you – or any of your cohorts of bureaucracy who reply-all – do actually want me to get something done, out of spite I'm just going to carry on playing my replica Pac-Man game for a while rather than responding. Maybe I'll throw in a couple of hands of poker and check out a bit of ratemypoo.com too. Then, when I finally do get around to dealing with your desperate plea for help, I shall be forced to condescend you. That's just the way it is, I'm afraid. Hey, you started it.

China

Uh-oh. Look out, world, here comes trouble.

Christmas

"Jingle bell, jingle bell, jingle bell rock…"

Oh, the dread.

Most people think *Jingle Bell Rock* is a cute little song to celebrate the rocking-ness of Christmas as epitomised by the jingling of bells on Santa's sleigh. Oh but it's not.

As everyone knows, a "jingle" is a catchy and annoying tune used for advertising; hence *Jingle Bell Rock* is quite clearly a warning that the bells on Santa's sleigh represent the approach of the season of gaudy commercialism and we should all dash our heads against rocks in anticipation of the pain it will inflict upon us. Also, "rock" almost rhymes with "kak". So that's got to be saying something right there.

And if you don't believe my interpretation of the song, just look at the sales figures: 100 million copies sold since it was released in 1957. Does money ever lie? Well, does it?

Anyway, just wait for the horrendous TV and print ads that start up in late October to get my drift: packets of sugar and lumps of margarine dressed up with tinsel and offered as "Christmas Price Busters". Followed shortly thereafter by tacky mall decorations and the endless recycling of horrendous Yuletide songs, as rehashed by Mariah Carey, Josh Groban and other ghastly pop singers who are bad enough as it is the rest of the year. How a December double-shift at Edgars doesn't turn the shop girls into raving loons, I don't know. And that's not even considering the hordes of maniac shoppers hurtling about the place, one of which, on the 24th of December at about 6pm, is invariably me, wondering how much I'll have to spend to alleviate the guilt and emotional blackmail of knowing that most of my presents were probably bought in early November. But not all of them. Clearly. What's with the "Homeboy Xtra" T-shirt, auntie Stella? I'm not 12 any more.

Wish I were though; the youngsters seem to be the only ones who can get through the season without suffering a nervous breakdown or drinking themselves into oblivion. More horrendous Christmas pudding, anyone?

P.S. Try getting *Jingle Bell Rock* out of your head now. I dare you. And it's one of the less painful Christmas songs…

Gareth Cliff

For some reason people don't complain that much about Gareth Cliff any more. Which is a bit odd considering he still comes across as a self-important, rude, smug, pompous, not-as-clever-as-he-thinks-he-is, world-class knob jockey.

But hey, disc jockey, knob jockey – maybe it's the same thing these days.

Hillary Clinton

Ever heard of David Icke? British writer, a bit unconventional. Believes a "Global Elite" of reptilian humanoids from the constellation Draco are trying to take over the world. George W Bush, the Queen, Tony Blair – all lizard people.

You can't be sure if Mr Icke, who only wore turquoise for a time, came up with this theory before or after the broadcasting of B-grade '80s alien-invasion show *V*, about a race of reptilian humanoids trying to take over the world, but you can be reasonably confident that he's a raging crazy.

But then you look at Hillary Clinton and you think, well, maybe he's on to something.

The Coconuts

Unfortunately, a lot of South African television programmes are… not good. So when an exceptional local show comes along we may be forced to concede that old chestnut that must make our TV producers writhe in dismay: "Not too bad – for something made in SA."

This begrudging compliment does not, however, apply to *The Coconuts*. Closer to the mark would be, "Way too bad – even for something made in SA."

Coke Zero

"Real Coke flavour, no sugar."

Except not really. Tastes more like Coke Light, I reckon.

The Competition Commission banking inquiry

It took them 22 months to complete the Competition Commission banking inquiry. In this time, according to reports, the inquiry panel "held 21 days of public hearings, conducted 101 stakeholder meetings and canvassed the views of a range of interested parties, including banks, consumer groups, small and prospective banks, non-banks and regulators". Sounds like a comprehensive effort. But they didn't canvass me – I'd say I qualify in the "non-bank" sector – and I could have done a better job in, oh, about two minutes.

Bank charges are too high, the inquiry concluded. It took them nearly two years and that's what they come up with. How about "too bloody high"? The last time I complained about this (see **Bank fees**, *Kak 1*), my bank, ABSA, was charging me a little over R200 a month in fees. When I looked the other day, it had magically risen to around R370, an 85 per cent increase in less than a year, without a word of warning or any explicable reason. Had I increased my transactions? Switched to a different payment system? Started using actual bank personnel to assist me rather than an already-established computer infrastructure? None of the above. ABSA evidently just decided that I needed to pay them more money. Little surprise to hear that transactional-fee income represents a third of South African banks' total income: R34.5 billion in 2006.

The inquiry also found that the setting of charges for bank customers' use of other banks' ATMs was "problematic" under the Competition Act. Problematic? How about "ridiculous and criminal"?

"We look forward to the continued co-operation of the banks to find solutions to these complex matters," said Competition Commissioner Shan Ramburuth. Like they're buddies. Like the banks give a second's thought to what the commission looks forward to.

"Hopefully now we will see a decrease in the cost of bank charges," said Thami Bolani, chairperson of the National Consumer Forum, in support of the Commission's findings. Thanks for that, Thami, but where's the outrage? Where's the open-jawed indignation at the fact that ABSA, FNB, Nedbank and Standard have been taking advantage of their clients for years now, contributing to cycles of consumer debt by charging ludicrous amounts on rejected debit orders and summarily upping fees without notification or justification? And we're not even touching on the credit mess they've helped create.

Some people like to blame George W Bush and the American credit crunch for South Africa's current economic malaise. But it would be wrong to let our banks off the hook. Fuckers.

Construction sites
They're everywhere! Can we please have some peace and quiet, for crying out loud? I can't sleep if I'm at home and I can't think if I'm at work!

I propose that there be no construction work on weekends, public holidays or between the hours of 5pm and 11am (because some of us sleep late). Or over lunch (say, 12.15pm till 2.30pm). And at nap time (from 3.30pm till 4.15pm).

I think you'll find that's pretty reasonable.

"Continuous partial attention"
A mildly irritating term defining the majorly irritating modern computer-related phenomenon of doing several things at the same

time without focusing on any of them, resulting in the virtual elimination of "complete and undivided attention" in modern society.

So when you're talking to a mate at the bar and he's keeping an eye on his cellphone just in case someone SMSes – that's continual partial attention. And when you're explaining something to a colleague and she's surreptitiously checking her email – same thing. And when you just can't get your work done because you're surfing the net, playing solitaire, MSNing and watching the cricket at the same time…

Huh? Where was I?

Cosatu's decision to march against high food prices and Eskom's incompetence

Does food listen? Does Eskom?

For Cosatu's information, the answers are "No" and "It's the government's fault". Which is to say that this particular march (in July 2008) was a general waste of time. Not only did it cost the economy somewhere in the region of R200 million, thus contributing to the current spiral of economic woe, but it cost all those who participated their daily wage. Except the organisers, of course – because they get paid to come up with and execute harebrained ideas like this. Indeed, a cynic might argue that the Cosatu gang leaders were just doing it as a justification for their monthly salaries. After all, if they weren't representing on behalf of the workers then they would have far less reason to charge union fees.

Another thing: did Cosatu really have to encourage our teachers to strike? Surely, if there's one thing we can agree on it's that we need desperately to educate the children of this country? The future Julius Malemas and co? Perhaps when the Cosatu honchos organise another pointless bit of mass action to endear themselves to the masses, they could at least leave the teachers out of it? Just a thought. (See **Zwelinzima Vavi**.)

Credit-card-reward schemes

Spend inordinate amounts of money on your credit card and we'll reward you with something from our incredibly large selection of really lame products! Free toaster once you've dropped R250K? How about a couple of bottles of cheap wine and a basket of soaps? Or go the frequent-flyer-miles option and after half a decade of setting fire to your wallet you may well earn yourself a Joburg-Cape Town one-way ticket. But only if you've managed to spend enough every year and carried the accumulated points over. (Tuesday-night flights only.)

How about no reward scheme and half the interest you're charging me? Because, you know, that debt is really killing me…

Crime and corruption

We've objected to it before, we're objecting to it now and – because this country verily dazzles with unbridled larceny, unpunished felonies and unadulterated dishonesty – we'll keep on objecting until someone, preferably a politician with some influence, actually does something about it. Not holding our breaths though.

Tom Cruise

Tom Cruise is, apparently, an Operating Thetan 6 in the Church of Scientology, which was started in the 1950s by L Ron Hubbard, a science-fiction writer widely reported to have discussed plans for inventing a religion to make money. Cruise evidently believes that an evil alien dictator by the name of Xenu, head of the Galactic Confederacy at the time, brought billions of his people to earth about 75 million years ago and blew them up with hydrogen bombs, and today the essence of these beings remain floating about the world infecting modern humans with negative energies.

I'm not buying it, though.

I believe that Cruise *is* Xenu. You look at that shit-eating grin and tell me he's human. *War Of The Worlds*? He was thinking, "Been here, done that."

D

Debonairs boerewors-encrusted pizza

Boerewors belongs on a braai and occasionally in a frying pan. Occasionally. Like when there's a hurricane outside. Or when there's no available wood, briquettes or charcoal within a hundred-mile radius.

Boerewors never belongs in the crust of a pizza. Never ever. Boerewors in the crust of a pizza is sacrilege. It is a violation of our cultural heritage. Why not burn the national flag while you're at it?

Ah, but I haven't tried it, have I? No. And I haven't tried a guacamole enema either. Or banging Rosie O'Donnell. Some things you just know.

Delivery drivers

Some excellent news for Bernie Ecclestone, who can breathe a sigh of relief and stop fretting about finding drivers for his next Formula One team: they're here in South Africa! Thousands of them! Daredevils, speed junkies and trick drivers, all delivering goods across the land and all itching for the opportunity to race Magny-Cours or Monaco.

Here comes your average delivery driver right now. His name's

Jerome, and he's off to drop off a piano. Nyyoooooooww! There goes Jerome.

And here comes Philemon. Nyyoooooooww! There goes Philemon.

If you travel behind Philemon at speeds approaching the sound barrier (as he hurtles down Main Road with Mrs Rosenkowitz's new washing machine sliding all over the place in the back), you may have enough time to read the contact number below his How's My Driving? sticker. But chances are you'll miss it. So you won't know who to phone to sign him up for the next F1 season – or to complain that he's dispatched your wing mirror to eternity while squeezing between your car and an oak tree without getting out of fifth gear.

South African delivery drivers refuse to be restrained by size or road surface any more. Whether it's a flower-carrying Datsun bakkie weaving through traffic or a cement truck barrelling down a residential lane, these guys are up for any vehicle on any track. Even Golden Arrow bus drivers are trying their damndest to earn a spot on the starting grid now, taking tips from their minibus-taxi heroes by cutting queues and straddling yellow lines. Use the entire track, seems to be the theory.

So what do you think, Bernie? Interested?

Pieter de Villiers's moustache

And his general dress sense.

Pieter, you seem like a decent enough person. You've got some interesting ideas and a grand plan of sorts (though I'd prefer you to implement it sooner rather than later), and so I wish you the best of luck. You're going to need it with our fickle crowds and abominable sports administrators (see **Booing rugby fans** and **Meddling sports administrators**). But I'm guessing you've realised that by now.

In the meantime, we need to do something about your appearance. So I'm recommending a stint on *Queer Eye For The*

Straight Guy to sort you out from top to toe. Either that or get some fashion advice from someone like Beast Mtawarira. He has flair.

Then maybe work on your public speaking. You're sounding disturbingly like the George W Bush of sport. "I know dancing is also a contact sport, but rugby is far from dancing. If you want to run with the big dogs then sometimes you have to lift your leg." Come again?

And this: "The same people who threw their robes on the ground when Jesus was on the donkey are the same people who crowned him and hit him with sticks. But they're also the same people who said they shouldn't have done that afterwards because he really was the Son of God… but I'm not saying I'm God."

No, Pieter, you're not God. God has a beard. And a nice white robe. A sort of classic-antiquities look. Not really your vibe.

Directory enquiries

Who do you call when you need a number? Do you give 1023 a try where, after a painful wait to speak to someone (see **Hold music**), you're in as much danger of being cut off as a foreskin at a bris? Or do you try an inaudible operator at your cellular network's directory enquiries? If it's the second option, you will invariably be reduced to guessing what she's saying, rattling off the name of the place you need, complete with spelling, and saying "SMS please" after an appropriate pause – then hoping she doesn't hit the wrong button and send it to the space shuttle. I'd like to be having it, please.

Disembarking

After enduring the hell of checking in, the humiliation of passing through security and the horrors of the flight itself, half of which served as a reminder of why you'll remain forever childless, another air-travel trial to add to the list comes at the other end: getting off the plane. In this instance it's not ACSA or the airline personnel who are the problem, it's your fellow passengers. Herewith a few tips when disembarking, fellow passengers.

Firstly, hold on just one minute after touch down before you turn on your cellphones. Please. Just one minute. Not that it's going to make any material difference to anything in the universe that you're breaking the quite explicit commands from the crew – the plane's not suddenly going to wheel out of control and crash into a fully laden bowser setting the airport alight, and whoever it is who's waiting for your SMS is not going to die in anticipation of your confirmed arrival – but just stop being so goddamned self-involved for a second.

Next, calm it down a bit when the time comes to get your luggage out of the overhead compartment. No need to leap from your seat like you're racing Le Mans, because they're still not going to let you off the plane until the stairs have arrived.

And finally, when the stairs do eventually arrive – in Cape Town this may take a while – and the queue starts moving, please be civil and go with the internationally accepted convention of filing off an aeroplane. That is, row by row. If I'm coming out of the row and you're in the aisle behind me, you have to wait. *Capiche?* Because next time you try to push in, I may just have to put a cap in your ass.

The disbanding of the Scorpions

Does anyone, anyone at all, including the staunchest Jacob Zuma-supporting, brainless ANC Youth League minion, doubt that the Scorpions were targeted for termination for the sole reason that they have investigated too many scandal-ridden upper-echelon governmental types, and one in particular?

No? Didn't think so. I guess the fact that the resolution to disband the unit took place a heartbeat or two after JZ was voted into the ANC presidency at Polokwane kind of gave it away.

DJs who play the music too loud

One of the explanations for this maddening phenomenon is that deafness is an occupational hazard of the DJing trade*. Another is that DJs are all giant egomaniacal douche bags. Whichever it is, I'm paying your freaking fee, you badly dressed, stringy-haired freak, so if I ask you nicely to turn down the volume just a tad because it's 9.15pm and people still want to talk a bit, then turn down the freaking music. And because it's my birthday, I'd like to listen to music *I* like, not music *you* like. I don't care if it's the Tiesto remix, no Justin bloody Timberlake!

This line of argument may work for five minutes if you're at a private party and you really are footing the bill, but in your local News Cafe, where the DJ thinks he is the absolute shit and the crowds are there only to hear him spin tracks, you've got more chance of Elton John walking through the door and fly-kicking him in the head. Which would be cool. But isn't going to happen.

* Just as the mercury-poison-related psychosis that afflicted hatters in the 19th century led to the adoption of the phrase "mad as a hatter", I'm thinking "deaf as a DJ" is ripe for addition to the modern lexicon.

Drivers who scoot up your arse just as you're about to parallel park

You've been missioning around town for what seems like half a lifetime trying to find parking when finally a car pulls out of a space in front of you so, punching the air with joy, you pull up in front of the spot, hit it into reverse and look over your shoulder – to see some goon in a bakkie three centimetres from your back bumper staring wide-eyed and gesticulating for you to hurry up and get out of his way. With your indicator blinking brightly and reverse lights engaged, not to mention the conspicuously open parking spot to his immediate left, it is patently obvious what your intentions are, and yet there he is – not entirely to your surprise – wide-eyed and gesticulating.

There are three obvious explanations for people driving up your arse while you're trying to parallel park. There is the small possibility that they weren't really concentrating on the road and suddenly found themselves there, in which case common sense and road courtesy would suggest they express a measure of embarrassment as they apologetically back up to wait for you. Or they could be colossally stupid, to the point that the flashing indicator, reverse lights and open parking bay don't add up to an imminent parallel-parking situation in their minds – but even the densest of South African road users will work out what's going on after you've made several pointing motions. Then there's the third option, the prize driving doos, whose combination of arrogance and inconsiderateness leads him to believe that if he manages to scoot up to your bumper before you've actually started reversing then you are obliged to give up and look for a space elsewhere. Never mind waiting six seconds for you to park or, god forbid, going around, your man thinks he owns the road, and when you've stubbornly faced him off – because the idea of looking for another spot is inciting murderous thoughts – and he deigns to drive around you, he will no doubt hoot for good measure. Like the tosser that he is.

Sadly, though, there is a fourth category. This is the guy who darts up your bottom defying any notion of common human decency in an almost inconceivably unconscionable attempt to force you on your way and thieve your hard-earned spot from under your nose. Yes, unfortunately drivers like this exist. You also find them cutting in at backed-up off-ramps (see **SA Drivers**, *Kak 1*) and driving in the emergency lane in rush-hour traffic (see **Minibus taxis**, *Kak 1*). And ultimately – we hope – in the seventh circle of hell.

Drivers yakking on their cellphones

The notion that women are excellent multitaskers can be disproved with one common example: the sight of a Sandton mommy in her bus-sized 4x4 trying to negotiate her way through an underground parking lot while trading goss with a girlfriend on the phone. If you're not convinced as you observe her veering towards unwary shoppers pushing trolleys to their cars or seeing the traffic back up after she pulls up at the boom and has to open her door, while still on the phone naturally, to reach across and insert her ticket, just watch her trying to get through the traffic circle down the road after she finally makes it out of there (see **Traffic circles**). And this isn't even with a couple of unruly rug rats on the back seat.

Busted, girls! Proof that you can't do 12 things at once... Or, at the very least, that you can't drive properly and hold a phone to your ear at the same time.

But that's not to claim that men are capable of doing it. The only dual-task we can perform is dropping off a number two and reading the newspaper at the same time. And actually we don't *really* do them at the same time... Suffice it to say the law stipulating that you may not pilot your car and talk into your cellphone simultaneously is a good one and should be obeyed by one and all.

As for text-messaging while bombing down Hospital Bend at 110km/h in your Nissan Micra, that's just dumb. Darwin will get you.

Dubya's lack of comedic form

What's the point of George W Bush if we aren't laughing at him? Remember these?

"Families is where our nation finds hope, where wings take dream."

"Rarely is the question asked: is our children learning?"

"I know how hard it is for you to put food on your family."

"They misunderestimated me."

Beautiful, Dubya. Beautiful. Timeless even. But old. Where's the new material, pardner?

For some reason Bushisms aren't making headlines any more. What's going on? It's not like he's magically gone and grown himself a brain, so we can only assume that he still puts his foot in his mouth at every available opportunity. And he's the president of America (astonishing as that fact still is), so he's got plenty of opportunities. But he's just not getting the coverage like he used to. No choking on pretzels, no falling off his bike, not even a "Yo Blair". Perhaps the Yanks are a little embarrassed about the fact that they've gone and voted into office a somewhat dim gentleman not once, but twice*, and think that if they ignore him now he may just go away. Or at least stop making a mess of the free world for a while. So the only news we've been picking up from the US since late 2007 is the race to see who'll replace him. Which, though it gives us hope for the future, just isn't funny.

"They misunderestimated me." Kills me every time.

* The appropriate Bushism here is, I believe, the legendary "Fool me once, shame on – shame on you. Fool me – you can't get fooled again…"

DVD fines

Bloody hell! Two days overdue and I may as well have just bought the thing.

No wonder illegal downloading is so popular.

E

The E! channel

What do you do when you've finished reading your weekly *heat* magazine? Why, you turn on E!, of course! It's the same thing, only on TV! Look! It's E! News giving you all the latest on JT, Brit, Christina and all the other celebs we're on a first-name basis with. Now over to Denise Richards in *It's Complicated*, telling us how complicated her life is. Which it isn't really. She just needed some extra money. And there are the Lohans in *Living Lohan* which, you'll be amazed to know, is not actually about the famous daughter, Lindsay. Rather, it's about the not-famous daughter Ali, who is trying to be famous. Not to forget Kim Kardashian, who doesn't even have a famous relative to cash in on but is trying her luck anyway, perhaps because her arse looks a bit like J Lo's. That would be on *Keeping Up With The Kardashians*. So you know.

E!'s full name, in case you haven't been told, is Entertainment Television. You probably wouldn't have been able to guess that from watching the channel, given that the entertainment value is appallingly low and that's it's merely a vacuous celebration of celebrity junk culture. They've even managed to ruin *Playboy*. Here's *The Girls Of The Playboy Mansion*: blonde bimbos keen to show their boobies, right? 'Fraid not. It's just blonde bimbos keen to talk about their feelings. But I don't want to hear them talk. I want to see their boobies. Where are the boobies?

E-filing

Is it just me or are the guys at SARS really starting to push their luck? First they have the temerity to shake down the entire country and get us all paying our taxes (well, a lot of us), then they expect us to start e-filing. Now we're paying them *and* doing their jobs for them. And it's not like they make it easy on us. I don't have the first clue about submitting taxes and rather hoped the downloadable IRP5 form available from the SARS website would require my name and a rough estimate of my desired rebate before I could press send. I wouldn't know. I couldn't get past the registration page. And I may as well have had a crazy person on the helpline.

"Hi, can you assist me with an e-filing query?"

"I am the walrus! Coo-coo kachoo!"

"Right. Well thanks for not wasting my time. Guess I'll get my dodgy accountant in again."

R150 to file my taxes! Money well spent, even if he's robbing me blind.

Electioneering

And 2009 general elections, here we go – a painful half-year of shameless politicking to look forward to…

Six months of insincere smiling faces looking down from lamp posts; six months of boring, repetitive radio spots that no-one really believes anyway; six months of promises waiting to be broken; six months of allegations of improper and underhand electioneering tactics; six months of improper and underhand electioneering tactics…

JZ trying to convince everyone how straight-down-the-line he is… The ANC Youth League trying to assure us that their specially commissioned election song *Hondo* (translation: *War*) is not about war or inciting violence… Mango Buthelezi trying not to lose any more support... Helen Zille (with arms crossed looking like she's auditioning for *CSI*) trying to persuade us she knows how to beat crime... Lekota and Shilowa doing their best to convince us that COPE isn't just a collection of recently retrenched opportunists...

You know what our politics needs? If we can't have an honest, incorruptible, competent leader with appropriate struggle credentials canvassing us for our votes, that is? We need someone who doesn't scare our pants off when we see his face on TV or party posters. Someone good-looking even. I'm thinking Loyiso. Or the guy from *Jacob's Cross*.

Email signatures

Herewith, an apparently necessary edict.

Six rules of the email signature:

1. Relax on the information overload. (Honestly, a job title and phone number will do – don't need your bra size.)
2. There is no need to include your email address. (Just how dim are the people you email?)
3. No attachments, please. (They really are unnecessary and my Outlook Express is soooo slow these days.)
4. Specifically, no attachment of your written signature. (Unless you're the chairman of the Reserve Bank. Then it's fine.)
5. Lose the legal mumbo-jumbo. ("Emails are not necessarily secure" – you don't say?)
6. And the motivational quote. (It's just preachy. No-one likes preachy.)

There. Much better.

The enduring legacy of HIV/Aids denialism

Remember when the whole Aids denialism debacle brought such shame and embarrassment upon our health ministry and the government in general? When the crackpot theory that HIV doesn't cause Aids and that antiretrovirals were the evil work of "pharmaceutical colonialism", as spouted by Matthias Rath and other universally discredited scientific dissenters, was taken seriously by President Thabo and Health Minister Manto? Rather than taking medicine that could prolong your life, head off to one of Mr Rath's workshops and buy his books and a course of vitamin therapy, was their message. Or just tuck into an African potato or beetroot...

Wow. It's almost surreal to think how many thousands of babies contracted the HI virus and how many tens of thousands of lives were lost prematurely as a result of our government's inability to implement a sound (and morally ethical) Aids policy for so many years. Thank god those days are over. Right?

Actually not. While Cabinet officially conceded in 2002 that HIV does, in fact, cause Aids and voted to make ARVs available nationwide in 2003, five years later doctors at Manguzi Hospital in KwaZulu-Natal (the South African and possibly world epicentre of the HIV crisis) were being censured by KZN MEC for Health Peggy Nkonyeni for issuing dual-therapy ARV treatments to pregnant mothers. Following World Health Organization guidelines and using international funding, Dr Colin Pfaff introduced dual antiretroviral prophylaxis into the hospital – and began saving lives as a result. This, according to Peggy and her crew, was a very naughty thing to do.

Meanwhile, as recently as May 2008, the censorious Peg was still hosting "HIV information workshops" from which Treatment Action Campaign representatives were barred and to which a colourful selection of Aids denialists and dissenters were invited. One of them, Zeblon Gwala, has been making something of a name for himself in KZN, selling a cure-all potion, the contents of which were apparently revealed to him in a dream, to HIV sufferers and discouraging them from taking their ARVs. Keynote speaker at the event was none other than Health Minister Manto – she really is an evil little troll, that woman – and the literature was of course provided by the Matthias Rath Foundation. A notable example of the advice on offer claimed that Aids drugs are "toxic and cause damage to the liver, the brain, the bone marrow and other organs" – the logic seemingly being that we wouldn't want to risk liver damage by saving lives. How Manto reconciles this line of thinking with her own liver issues is a bit of a wonder.

Energy-efficient light bulbs

They're well-intentioned, energy-efficient light bulbs. No denying it. Global warming and incompetent Eskom and all that. But just look at the alternatives: the warming radiant glow of a normal light bulb or a depressing soul-destroying blue gloom that you can't read a newspaper headline by? Maybe if you live in an underground parking lot you'll be happy with the blue, but once you've worked out that energy-efficient bulbs reduce power-grid consumption by feeding directly on the human spirit, you'll realise that simply stopping commuting is the superior energy-saving option. If anyone calls to find out why you're not at work you can blame it on the environment.

Estate agents' jargon

Designer Kitchen. Kitchen remodelled within the last five years, not necessarily by a designer called Antonio from Euro la Spec, more likely by some guy who shops at Hennie's Wholesalers in Industria Park. But add on half million to the sale price anyway.

Sparkling Pool. A pool, but better. Look carefully at any patch of water on a sunny day, even at a sewerage farm, and an estate agent will see it sparkle. Add on R300,000.

Tuscan. Used to mean "from Tuscany". Now means a house that doesn't have gutters and is painted baby-vomit brown or thereabouts. South Africans *love* Tuscan. Even if it's actually Brakpan facebrick overlooking a railway station.

Urgent Sale. Usually comes with a story: "Shame, the poor guy who owns the house just broke up with his fiancée and moved back to Sweden…" and they've just rezoned the Gautrain through your back yard.

Renovator's Dream. A piece of crap. Drop Anglo American's annual turnover on top of the sale price and it might be livable.

Close To Nature. Imminent land claim next door.

Architect-designed. Vital. As opposed to – what? – aardvark-designed?

A nice, honest real-estate business would really be a breath of fresh air. They could go by the name Call-it-like-it-is Properties. Tag line: "You'll hate us slightly less than other real estate agents."

Ethnic categorisation

It's not just about black and white any more; it's ethnicity too. So you're only "African" enough if you're properly black. You know, black black. Not charcoal, not midnight blue. Black! Coloured people just don't count any more. Which is odd considering that the Khoi and San were here first… Although that's entirely besides the point, of course, because you're going to struggle to find a white South African who doesn't see himself as African. (The clue is in the term "South *African*".)

And anyway, I'm coloured. Seriously, there is a touch of the tar brush in the family. I swear it. How are you going to prove me wrong? Pencil test? Or shall we just dig up all those old apartheid records and use those?

F

Facebook

Facebook, Fakebook, Fistbook, Vleisbook, Stalkbook, Fuckbook – whatever you call it, social networking online is the abomination of modern living. Really, it is. Do we even have to discuss this?

How collectively insecure have we become that we have to be "friends" with people we went to school with but haven't seen in 14 years? And hope for invites to parties we don't have any intention of attending from ex-colleagues we used to work with last century? And play Super Mario Bros with people we haven't even met before? And tell the world, via our status bars, that we've had a very long day and feel like soup for dinner?

And then there's poking people. The most vacuously arbitrarily superficially insipidly lame thing a person can do. And "Hey, long time, what you up to?" messages.

"Not much. You?" You twat.

The fasten-seatbelt alarm

Besides the interest rates (see **Interest rates**), the prime reason for not trading in your 1988 Golf II for a new Audi A3 is that crazy-making pinging that sounds when you pull off for the 30-second drive to the corner café. Insanity for your ears.

Fat people who complain about their weight

Okay, so there's the remote possibility you have a thyroid problem, in which case I sympathise. But no-one's buying the "slow metabolism" excuse. Chances are you're sucking down Twinkies under your desk between brunch and lunch, and supersizing your McDonald's shakes. Here's some advice, fatties: move a little more, eat a little less.

Ferrari Formula One fans

Unathletic geek wannabes with no hand-eye coordination, whose proudest possession is either a nylon Ferrari jacket or a Ferrari bumper sticker on the back of a crappy old Opel Kadett. Go play *Dungeons And Dragons*, you Tifosi losers.

FHM covers

Must! There! Be! So! Many! Gratuitous! Exclamation! Marks?! At last count – October 2008 – there were 28 of the little bastards on the cover of South African *FHM*, excluding the *Collections* inset. And for once I'm not even exaggerating. For God's sake, aren't men reading this magazine? Or is it just 14-year-old boys with sweaty palms?

The (as yet unproven) Fidentia crimes

Hypothetically speaking, if J Arthur Brown and his Fidentia cohorts are found guilty by the courts, you've got to wonder about the human race. What goes on in a man's head that he can deliberately choose to con thousands of widows and orphans (among others) out of their living allowances? Perhaps the only way to make sense of it is to assume the mindset of conniving financial con artist. Here's how my thought processes might go:

Right. So I'm running my financial services company and I feel it's time to "acquire" some more money. I've got a fair bit already but I'm feeling good for a couple of hundred million more. Wifey has her nice little day spa to run and I've got four mansions and six Ferraris, but I figure I need another cabinet of Rolexes and maybe a pile of diamonds and rubies to swim in – so who's next in the cross hairs? Some big-business wheeler-dealers who've got so much money they don't know what to do with it? A government department trying desperately to throw away its allocated budget? Some middle-class suckers looking to make a quick buck? No no, none of that really excites me...

I know, how about some miners' widows and orphans? I only have to go for the really poor ones who are literally struggling to put food in their mouths and are desperate for the couple of hundred rand a month they get from their measly pension plans. Cool idea! And after that I can try drowning some puppies and skywriting "Hey kids, Father Christmas isn't real!" over major metropolitan areas. Then maybe I can attach some kittens to broomsticks and polish the marble floors of my gazebo. Awesome plan!*

Sick and depraved just about describes the mentality of a man who can happily allow himself to thieve (an estimated) R800 million from Eastern Cape peasants just so he can throw some more money on the pile. It also describes the mentality of murderous criminals who take it upon themselves to gang rape alleged fraudsters in the back of the prisoners' truck on the way to court. Hey! How about we arrange a meeting?

They say that the assault on J Arthur Brown turned out to be a big ol' lie so that he could make bail or get preferential treatment in jail, but wouldn't it have been great if it were true? What a nice lesson for prospective white-collar criminals that would've been.

* Just to confirm, that's all *my* thinking right there, not J Arthur's.

Forms

Ah, a UIF form. You'd think, as a vaguely intelligent and competent person, that you'd be able to fill in such a form with relative ease. At least without wanting to resort to tears. Or violence. Or tearful violence. And, of course, the dread in your hand as you reach for the pen would tell you just how wrong you are.

Whether it's a UIF requirement, an application at Home Affairs or even a cycle-race entry, forms these days all seem to require information you don't have while not requesting information you think they should have. There are miniscule spaces for big words, as though hand-microprinting the Bible onto the backs of postage stamps is what you do for a living, followed by four lines for single-word answers, so you feel all insecure and take several five-minute sessions over a period of two months to fill in the damn thing. Then you arrive somewhere with it and they say they need a photo or a fingerprint or your grandfather's signature from beyond the grave. Bastards!

Funky handshakes

This is a polite request to black men. Black men, please bear in mind when meeting a white man for the first time that, in the new South Africa, this occasion may well involve an element of insecurity for him. Chances are he'll be trying not to embarrass himself by saying anything racist or patronising, and he'll probably be thinking that you know people in government and if he doesn't make a good impression you might just get them to nationalise every company in the country or raise company taxes or something. And there's your big penis to worry about too.

So try to ease his worried mind when you shake hands. If you're going to do the triple-grip over-under handshake, you'll probably need to give him some kind of guidance. Or at least a warning. And don't even think of trying the clicking thing with the thumb. Not a chance he'll work it out.

G

Gas braais

In Australia there is a brilliant term that has been promoted by the government – and widely adopted by the public – to discourage certain unsavoury or unappreciated behaviours. The term is "unAustralian". So if you drop garbage out your car window, well, that's just unAustralian, mate. Want to duck off home without buying your round? No, mate – unAustralian. Celebrate Anzac day without playing a bit of two up and putting a fifty on the horses? You betcha, mate – unAustralian. Only Australians could come up with a word like this and get away with it. Well, maybe Canadians could too, but unAustralian is so Australian it's like a dingo stole my baby.

In South Africa, we couldn't be bothered with detail like this. We litter and bum off our friends and don't get too obsessed about gambling on public holidays because, well, we're big-picture people. We're more concerned with just staying alive. As a result, the term "unSouth African" is almost not applicable. Almost. There is one thing though: the gas braai.

A gas braai in South Africa is fundamentally and critically wrong. It is like James Bond driving a pink Mazda MX-5 or the Pope telling paedophile jokes. It's like Paris Hilton's parents'

decision not to abort. It's like that scene in *The Crying Game*…
Yes, that's just how wrong it is.

In South Africa the use of heated gas, as efficient and effective as it is, is no way for a man to prepare uncooked meats for human consumption when outdoors. Wood, charcoal or briquettes are the permissible fuels; *only* wood, charcoal or briquettes. This is because a braai is not just a means of preparing food. Far from it. A braai is an occasion. It is a ceremony. It is a communing of like-minded souls. And this takes time. How is a man expected to commune when he's halfway through his first Amstel and the steaks are already done? How is he supposed to bond with his brothers when he's had no opportunity to comment on the impressive heat intensity generated by the braai master's coals, and speculate on the time at which he believes those coals will be ready for cooking? How is he meant to feel at one with the land under his feet and the world all around him until the game has been fully analysed, the Johnny Clegg CD has played through at least once and he has had several opportunities to carefully and dutifully monitor the chops and boerie while the braai master has slipped off for a pee?

Indeed, we may as well ask, how can a man be a man without a braai?

The gay-induced Anglican schism

In case you haven't been following what's going on in religious circles – because you've been really busy, or your internet connection was down, or you couldn't really care less – there have been some heaven-and-earth-shattering events occurring in the Anglican church of late. No longer is it one united religion as we used to know it, spiritually led from on high by the revered Archbishop of Canterbury. Uh-uh, girlfriend! The gays are causing havoc!

Indeed, a great Anglican schism appears to be taking place, due mainly to fundamentalist Old Testament sticklers taking issue with the Anglican Communion's increasing liberalism, in particular its decision not to ostracise homosexuals as a guiding doctrine. So, very roughly put, there are those who are happy to ordain gay bishops in one camp, and there are the moffie bashers (who presumably aren't very comfortable with this camp talk) in the other.

Wow! Aren't these rebellious religious leaders something? Happy to tear apart their entire belief system because of a private issue that seldom, if ever, directly affects them. So narrow-minded that they can't resolve a minor Biblical interpretation, and yet still with moral and life-guiding influence over millions of people…

What do you suppose goes on in their heads when they're alone at night? Do they envision the forthcoming rapture with the Antichrist appearing as a lipstick-smeared cross-dressing fagmosexual? Do they foresee an apocalypse featuring hordes of chest-waxed vest-wearing A-list gaylords roaming the streets listening to Mika? Will there at least be a couple of murderers and child molesters as well? Or is it just the gays?

Weirdos. Probably all in the closet.

Getting older

One day you wake up to the realisation that Linkin Park isn't actually the best background music in the world and you are, in fact, rather partial to the pleasant esoteric beats of Delerium, featuring the melodious voices of Sarah McLachlan, Jacqi Hunt and others. Round about this time, you may also begin to notice that 19-year-old girls no longer look at you with a glint in the eye; instead, they look at you like you're a paedophile. Then you develop an allergic reaction to beer and get a bad back. What's next? Adult nappies and dinner at 4pm? Bloody hell, I'm only 30!

Gillette's 5-blade Fusion razor

I remember back when twin blades were introduced. That was revolutionary, man. Instead of one blade, there were… two. Things would never be the same after that. Hell, the world would never be the same after that. Then, no-one really knows how, but Gillette came up with the Mach 3. Not just two blades – no no, three blades! We were scared to try it at first but then we did and it was, like, whoa. But it was better than whoa. It was like you'd shaved and replaced your face skin with a baby's ass. A baby's ass! But in the end that wasn't enough. We needed more. So Wilkinson Sword brought together the world's greatest minds – were they composing symphonies, solving perpetual motion, explaining string theory? Forget it, baby, they were combining their genius to come up with the Schick Quattro. Quattro means four in Latin and that was truly pushing the envelope. People said it was dangerous, that it couldn't be done, but they did it. And now… well, Gillette has deployed the world's largest supercomputers and with futuristic technology that writes military code and maps galaxies they have – whisper it – invented a five-blade razor. Yes. Five blades. My god, what can't they do?

Come back in 50 years and you'll probably find a 700-blade razor. Or just sheer unadulterated madness.

Girlfriends' dreams in which their boyfriends are being nasty to them

I didn't do it, woman! It was in your head! Stop being so pissed off with me!

Government shock at South African crime statistics

In August 2008 deputy minister of justice Johnny de Lange admitted in a report to Cabinet that the South African criminal justice system was "fragmented and dysfunctional". The crime stats, bad enough as they are – 50 murders a day, 100 rapes, 650 burglaries – do not reflect the true situation in the country, because many of us can't be bothered even to report crime. Detectives are hugely understaffed and can't investigate many crimes, let alone catch and convict the criminals. The state employs about 2,000 forensic scientists who must deal with more than 600,000 contact crimes a year. The statistical records and computer systems are in "the Stone Age" – so out of date that crimes that occurred five years ago can't be tracked. They have no access to the (extensive) fingerprint database at the Department Of Home Affairs. In a word, the criminal justice system is completely-utterly-fucked.

For once, being right – as the entire South African population, begging for the government to sit up and take note, has been all along – is no consolation. We just want something done about it. The fact that Thabo "down to earth" Mbeki and various ministers were "shocked" by this news defies comprehension. Why was this? Because they didn't bother to listen to people in the streets? Didn't watch the news? Didn't read newspapers – even newspaper headlines?

Whatever the reasoning, there can't have been too many victims of crime who were particularly upset about the T-boss's ousting and fall from grace the following month. Joyous celebrations in the street, more like.

Grey's Anatomy

You may have heard of the phrase "jump the shark". It's what happens when a previously entertaining TV show takes the plunge from entertainment greatness to viewing dross, a point in time that is often reflected in one moment of sheer television implausibility that suggests the writers have run out of ideas and will do anything to keep the pay cheques rolling in. As in the episode of *Happy Days* when the Fonz, played by Henry Winkler and wearing his trademark leather jacket, leapt over a shark while water-skiing.

Other classic shark-jumping moments:

• *Knight Rider* – when good KITT and evil KARR turbo-boosted themselves into a midair collision. Can't remember how they resurrected KITT after that one…

• *Airwolf* – when the entire cast of Airwolf was replaced in its fourth season. They even resorted to using old footage of Airwolf…

• *The A-Team* – when they made an armoured car out of a shoe box, a record player and some used toilet roll. Oh wait, they did that in every episode.

These days, television shows that have jumped the shark have an easy tell: their all-gloss no-substance marketing imagery for the ad breaks and DVD box covers invariably look like a *Vanity Fair* studio shoot, complete with Zoolander-esque model poses, perfect make-up and a month's worth of air-brushing. Conversely, respectable shows with a bit of integrity left tend to stick to bog-standard on-set photos that actually resemble the characters and imply more importance being given to story lines and character development.

Not sure what I'm on about? Just think of the first few seasons of *Friends* when it was a genuinely funny sitcom – ad break: everyone having fun – versus its last few seasons when they all took themselves very seriously and it became so unbearable that you wanted to leap out the nearest window on hearing the intro music – ad break: portrait pictures of individual characters posing for Annie Leibovitz. Grrrr.

Which all brings us to *Grey's Anatomy*, the one show we used to be able to watch with our girlfriends without feeling too emasculated. Or like killing ourselves. Admittedly the girls were all a tad hysterical about it, but we had to concede there was some genuinely okay scriptwriting going on – for the first season or so... Now we have whiny, neurotic Meredith in unashamed Blue Steel half-pout or wimpy Patrick McSpineless with mousse hair and middle-distance gaze segueing into numerous and lengthy ad breaks – sure-fire indicators of the rubbish-soap-opera melodrama that a show must descend to so its network can squeeze out every last dollar. Why the producers can't display some creative integrity and call it a day when the plot lines run dry is a mystery. Well, not really. It's the money thing I've just mentioned. (Just look at shameless spin-off *Private Practice*, which at least had the decency to be shit right from the start.) Still, if only they followed the British lead. *The Office*: 14 episodes. *Fawlty Towers*: 12 episodes.

Done and done. Classics forever.

Other incriminating jump-the-shark moments:

- Someone dies but is miraculously revived, usually after experiencing a supernatural event and/or communing with the dead, and with no further medical complications. *Grey's Anatomy*, check.

- The most interesting character is written out of the show because of an off-screen issue. *Grey's Anatomy*, check.

- An arbitrary addiction appears out of the blue (frequently developing in just one episode. You know, like most addictions). *Grey's Anatomy*, check.

- Various characters have sex. *Grey's Anatomy*, check check check.

- A barrel-scraping meaningless lesbian kiss occurs. *Grey's Anatomy*, check. (See **Attention-seeking faux-lesbian kissing**.)

And let's not forget the plinky plonky time-to-laugh music (see **"Funny" music on TV shows, *Kak 1***) and touching, soppy time-to-cry pop songs that indicate to viewers exactly which heartstring is being tugged, or the moralising voice-over that no-one listens to, or the soapie plot lines…

Someone's got to break it to the chicks: *Grey's Anatomy* is a steaming pile. In fact, I refuse to watch it. Unless you ask really nicely. And you don't complain about my sarky comments. Or when I make armpit-fart sounds. Or when I want to watch *South Park*.

H

Hadedahs

Birds. I'm generally cool with them. They're usually quite pretty and they often make pleasant chirping sounds. But not all of them.

Hadedahs, for example, are an ornithological atrocity. They live for one thing and one thing only: making a nuisance of themselves. Whether it's a midnight flyover or a 6am threesome in the oak tree outside my window, these bald-headed Pinocchio-nosed flying vagrants can't do anything without screeching like a sackful of dying cats. It's enough to drive you homicidal.

Where did they come from anyway? Fifteen years ago you hardly found a hadedah in Cape Town; you only ever saw them when you made the trip up north. Now they're everywhere, squadrons of noise pollution wheeling across the skies. Bloody Joburgers taking over this place. If this is the price we pay for global warming then I'm definitely getting rid of my iron smelter…*

And if it's not the hadedahs in the oak tree outside my bedroom at 6am, it's the goddamned randy Egyptian geese. Or the raucous guineafowl. I don't want any of this unruly birdlife in the oak tree outside my bedroom window at 6am, thank you very much. What I want is a Steller's sea eagle. Yes, that would be great. Open the curtain and there's a Steller's sea eagle. Although this is somewhat unlikely considering the majority of Steller's sea eagles live on the Kamchatka peninsula in south-eastern Russia. My second option, then, is a white eye.

Ah, a white eye.

Twitter twitter.

Now piss off and let me sleep.

---

* Although hadedah range expansion apparently has more to do with human development of previously unsuitable open spaces into golf courses, playing fields and the like. Ah.

Handymen, plumbers and DStv installers

The four-hour wait times and brazen efforts to rip me off are to be expected, along with likely attempts to steal my household goods. But I could live with all that if I didn't have to call them out for the same job two months later.

DStv installers are the worst of the lot. If you're lucky you'll only have to take two days off work before four of them descend on your house, tack up your satellite dish and charge you half your salary. Then winter arrives and it starts to rain, or the guy next door decides to install a zinc roof on his new garage, so your reception goes moggy and you can't watch TV without wanting to brain yourself, and you have to haul them back out again to prop the dish up on a 20-foot pole. Why couldn't they just do that in the first place? And why is DStv so expensive? And so crap? There's nothing to watch!

Happy birthday wishes sent via computer-generated SMS

Can there be any more damning example of modern-day cynicism than the computer-generated happy birthday message? Somewhere out there in the computer ether a collection of microchips registers a change in time and date, generates some code and fires it off to a server, and next thing you have an SMS saying, "Hi Tim Warm birthday greetings! From Atlantic Chiropracric Health Centre". You know what, rather don't send me a meaningless birthday greeting. Rather just fix my back. Instead of making it fractionally better for half a day. And fix your spelling too.

A couple of the more memorable SMSes from my last birthday:

"Dear Tim. Wishing you a very Happy Birthday from all of us here at Glasshouse!!!Hope you have a great day!!!"

Too late. Not with all those exclamation marks.

"Dear MR RICHMAN, AIG wishes you a Happy Birthday this month! We have a great offer for you, expect a call shortly."

Ooh ooh, a great offer, I can't wait for my unsolicited telesales pitch! And because these people remembered my birthday, they must really care about me… Except they didn't even text me on the right day.

Health "facts" that turn out to be a load of bollocks

Drink at least eight glasses of water a day. Great advice. If it wasn't completely without foundation – which scientists from the University of Pennsylvania worked out recently when they reviewed all studies published on day-to-day hydration. Turns out no-one knows where the idea came from, and unless you're clinically dehydrated you don't need the extra H_2O. Man, that's just annoying. All those years of unnecessary water consumption, all those pees we could have avoided.

But that's not the only untrue health "fact", as spouted by however many magazines and websites and people who think they know what they're talking about. Vitamin C as a cure for the common cold is equally baseless, it seems. And oily fish with its omega-3s may not be as great as we all think. But then again it may be. Who really knows? The guys in the white coats sure can't decide. Here's some research that suggests that something might cause something else, one of them says. And here's some other research into all that research that suggests it may turn out to be a load of balls, says another. Same thing with margarine and butter. One moment marge is the thing, the next it's butter. And they can't really say about drinking moderate amounts of red wine either. It may help ward off heart disease but it may increase the likelihood of cancer…

Whatever can we do? Looks like it's going to boil down to common sense. Drink water when you're thirsty, eat oranges and salmon because they're tasty, opt for butter because of its buttery goodness, and drink red wine in excess because, well, you never know. Maybe it doesn't destroy your liver and rot your brain.

N.B. Just to be clear, Thabo and Manto, HIV causes Aids. That one they're unanimous about.

Health and Safety

For all our complaints about life in South Africa – crime, corruption, the cost of living, yadda yadda – let us all thank whomever or whatever it is we thank when we're feeling particularly thankful that we don't live in England. The weather's one thing and the Poms themselves are quite another, but just consider for a moment having to deal with all that political correctness – a particularly large portion of which is used to issue Health and Safety directives. Nuts to that idea.

Health and Safety is what happens when people don't have to worry about their actual health and safety any more. If there is no urgent threat on your life – no hijacker in the bushes, no concerns about Aids or XDR tuberculosis – then it's time to stress out about the really small things that have a one-in-a-zillion chance of causing you or those around you harm.

In the UK nothing can happen without a platoon of H&S inspectors giving the all clear. Carpenters and woodworkers are instructed to avoid using brooms to sweep up wood chippings and sawdust for fear of asthma. Children may no longer use egg cartons to create models for risk of salmonella poisoning. Recently, a school banned sack racing to avoid the dreaded threat of pupils falling over; another banned knotted ties. At one university, students may no longer toss their academic caps in the air at graduation for fear that they may cause injury to themselves or others. And if you think that's bad, try working at the Health and Safety Executive, where employees are not even permitted to move office furniture; they have to arrange porters, who are expertly trained in the moving of tables and chairs, up to 48 hours in advance to do it for them. That's special.

But the UK is not alone. America, with its lawsuit culture, is right up there, of course: cups of hot coffee are labelled "Hot"*; chain saws come with warnings for users not to attempt to stop the blade with body parts; Kinder Surprise eggs are banned for fear of children eating the plastic toy inside. The Germans have also taken issue with the Kinder Surprise eggs; plus they want to make schoolbooks lighter so that pupils don't injure themselves or get tired carrying them around. In Australia and New Zealand, millions of dollars of taxpayers' money is spent on advertising that advises people not to brush their teeth too hard and road users to "brake before the bend"...

It's one of the happy side effects of living in South Africa, where health and safety is not a guaranteed luxury, that we can just be normal and survive on our common sense. It's evolutionary, it weeds out the morons, and it at least gives us an illusion of freedom. But there are signs. Ominous signs. Signs that the H&S fun succubus is sniffing around our shores. For example, if you worked at a particular government statutory body based in Pretoria in June 2008 you probably would have received a group email outlining the hazards of slipping and falling in the office. Here are the edited (but not copy-edited) highlights:

"Slips and Falls are most common office accidents, a falls occurs when you lose your balance or footing. The easiest way to avoid slips and falls is to pay attention to your surrounding and to avoid running or rushing... Be sure the pathway is clear before you walk... Avoid excessive bending, twisting and leaning backwards while seated... Chairs should never be used as ladders. Never carry anything that obscures your vision. Wear stable shoes with non-slip soles".

Amazingly, this email was not signed off by Captain Obvious. It is a genuine email communication sent with serious intent and which the reader was supposed to take seriously. And yet it includes an explanation of what it means to fall. And it instructs readers how to walk. And how to sit. Basic skills that most people master before they can – I dunno? – spell "patronising"... But forget the palpable condescension for a minute; it's the underlying intent to suck out the joy and glory of being alive from whomever is unfortunate enough to read the email – let alone the poor staff who are supposed to follow these instructions – that is most disturbing. Let us pray that this is not a harbinger of things to come. This country needs Health and Safety like I need a Swedish gonad massage.

* The infamous "McDonald's coffee case" in 1994 saw a jury in New Mexico award an 81-year-old woman $2.86 million in damages after she spilled hot coffee in her crotch and suffered third-degree burns. After appeal, the final settlement apparently worked out to around $600,000. Americans...

Hermanus

Once upon a time Hermanus was a peaceful little getaway just outside of Cape Town. Catch some waves, do a little fishing, have a braai. Good times. Then they chucked in a few restaurants and a couple of traffic lights and the times were still good, just a bit vibier. Then the property developers moved in. Those motherfuckers.

Now Hermanus is crap. Now, instead of quickly zipping out there for the weekend, you take an extended traipse into paradise lost, the last ten kilometres of which quite closely resemble driving through Randburg. Then you arrive in what was once a pleasant village square but is now an enclosure of fast-food joints and tacky souvenir shops, which smells like take-out and urine and is overrun with families wandering about in matching Cheetahs rugby jerseys or teenagers whose sole purpose in life seems to be to generate noise. It is a tragic tale like no other – what happens when you take a charming fishing town next to the sea and plonk Bellville on top of it. Oh, the injustice of it…

But wait! Perhaps there is hope! Because lurking beneath this nasty veneer of overexploitation, the heart of Hermanus still beats and the Hermanus patriots of yore await their moment to reclaim their town. One day soon they will rise up together to tear down the neon signs, bulldoze the flea market and napalm the golf-estate housing developments. Then the supermarkets and shopping complexes will be burnt to the ground, along with the liquor stores and the Wimpy and McDonald's and KFC, and Hermanus as we used to know it will return… Oh, it will be a most glorious day, buwa-buwahahahaha!

Except that's not going to happen.

Damn it.

P.S. If it does happen, just a polite request for them to leave the Italian deli. It's quite nice to have a croissant on a Saturday morning.

Hold music

Sometimes it's the Beatles' greatest hits on the panpipes. Or it could be a computer-generated *Für Elise*, as though Benny from *LA Law* is playing a glockenspiel in your ear. Occasionally you get reasonable sound quality of some '90s soft pop but just when you're getting into *Everything I Do*, they interrupt you with an ad for whatever new policy they happen to be selling. And then a "Your call is important to us" message. Lies! It's all lies! They're just getting their sadistic rocks off as we suffer the hold-music torture!

The Human Rights Commission

"Hear this, my people, those who I lead and blindly follow me: the world would be a better place if Julius Malema were dead. We should not shy away from killing him. Him and Zwelinzima Vavi."

"Um, excuse me, but you can't say that."

"What? You talking to me?"

"Er, no… I mean yes. You can't say those bad things. They're bad."

"Shut the hell up. I can do whatever I want."

"But they're really bad. That's hate speech. It could incite violence."

"Nonsense! Don't prescribe your liberal definition of language on me."

"No really, you should apologise. Or at least pretend to apologise."

"Oh come off it, I didn't actually mean 'kill', per se. I meant 'present with a bouquet of flowers'. Don't take me so literally!"

"Ohhh, a bouquet of flowers, right. That's okay then. Well, why don't you come in and sit down with us, in a month or two, say, and maybe we can discuss the issue a bit and, you know, not really do much about it… Please come in. Pretty please. Pleeeeaase… Pleasepleasepleasepleasepleaseplease…"

What's the point of the HRC again?

The I'm-offended bandwagon

Internationally, people who love to be offended tend to be one or more of the following: privileged, white, hippy, liberal, lesbian and, most importantly, not a member of the minority group in question. They also tend to blow things out of proportion. Take for example Martin Brundle's "pikey" comment in an ITV interview with Bernie Ecclestone at the Canadian Grand Prix in June 2008, which led to much wailing and gnashing of teeth as well as international headlines and official grovelling apologies from all concerned. This after UK broadcasting watchdog Ofcom and ITV received a total of 36 complaints. How many of those people were actual gypsies, do you think? Or even itinerant travellers? I'm guessing none. Because the gypsies probably realised Brundle had no intention of being offensive and they had better things to do.

In South Africa, the I'm-offended bandwagon jumpers have a slightly different agenda. Here, rather than simply looking to bolster their PC credentials, they seem to focus on playing the offended card – often race-related – either as an instinctive "right-thing-to-do" reaction to our guilt-ridden past or as a means to garner some kind of political high ground. Or both.

The outraged people and groups who wrote in to the Human

Rights Commission about Jon Qwelane's scandal-mongering gay-bashing column that seemed to suggest bestiality was the next level down from homosexuality spring to mind. How many of these people actually bought and read the piece in question – which was in the *Sunday Sun*, hardly your average homosexual's newspaper of choice – and were actively offended by it? As with the Brundle incident, I'd venture to guess a rather small minority. And the rest were? That's right, bandwagon jumpers. Because honestly, who gives a fuck what Jon Qwelane writes?

The impending doom of Mankind

Doom. It just has that delightful Revelations ring to it, doesn't it? Religious nuts have been predicting the end of the world every year since, well, since there have been religious nuts (an unfortunately long time). Now learned individuals are saying quite plainly that we are screwed. Scientist who have spent their careers applying their exceptional intelligence to the analysis of centuries of recorded data are concluding that, basically, it's too late: too late to stop climate change, massive loss of biodiversity, our still-exploding population, our depletion of the earth's biological capital, degradation of farmlands – the list goes on. This isn't to say our species is in jeopardy and we're all going to die tomorrow. On the contrary; it quite possibly won't affect you and me that much. But things are going to become decidedly kakker for us as a species. And our children are going to have even more reason to resent us.

The "impending doom of South Africa"

The entry above – that's real. On a grand scale mankind is truly screwed if you listen to the people who know what they're talking about. But South Africa... honestly, who knows?

The prophets of this country's doom have been around for decades, since the '70s and '80s, when the end of apartheid began looming on the horizon. Off to America and England

and Australia they went, predicting a landscape of mayhem just around the corner for those of us foolish enough to stay: civil war, blood in the streets, an economy in ruin... Then when Nelson Mandela was released from jail in 1990 the stock market took a dive and the rand dropped ten per cent in a heartbeat. And so more doom mongers emerged and packed their bags. But much to their dismay – as they watched from Vancouver or Perth or Auckland – the country didn't fall apart. And it didn't fall apart when the ANC won the elections in 1994, or five years later when Mandela stepped down and Thabo took over, or in 2001 when the rand went through the floor, or in 2004 when the ANC got a two-thirds majority allowing them to alter the constitution. In fact, not thaaat much has changed in the last 30 years. We still get by, we still bitch about the idiots in charge, we still have a jol.

And now, as Thabo gets used to unemployed life and JZ worms his way towards the top spot, the Nostrodamuses are once again at it, laying down their ghastly predictions – "the next Zimbabwe" is a current favourite. It's almost as though they *want* South Africa to fall apart – to justify schlepping across the world to Brisbane perhaps? Whether it happens now or later is neither here nor there for them. Because in 2187, when South Africa does finally come apart at the seams, when inflation maxes out and the cryogenically frozen Julius Malema returns to install himself as dictator for life, there they'll sit croaking with glee into their oxygen-replacement vats... "See? See? Told you so."

The Indian Premier League

How long did the Twenty20 IPL last? A year? What a bore... All those cricketing greats and Bollywood celebs and fireworks and last-ball finishes and cross-batted sixes – and basically it was a steaming load of elephant manure. In this case, Indian elephant manure. We just need some on-field umpire abuse and a couple of late-night team gang bangs to add to the faux glam and mercenary ruination of the game, and cricket will be the new soccer.

But how to summarise the competition neatly? Perhaps this from Kolkata Knight Riders franchise owner Shahrukh Khan will do the trick as an illustration of the delightful people behind the farce: "My team told me that they have yet to meet a better human being than me. This is a huge compliment."

That's about as apt as you could find in a two-sentence quote. Or there's this:

A waste. Of time.

The inordinate power of car manufacturers

One of the problems with being a motoring journalist in this country (besides the fact that you are a motoring journalist) is that they never let you get away with speaking your mind if you don't think that absolutely everything about the latest car is just fan-spiffy-tastic. Not too many call-it-like-it-is Jeremy Clarksons down here, that's for sure. Just you try taking the piss out of a wanky weekend launch for the latest Merc or Audi after all the other petrolhead hacks have been raving so they will be invited to the next do and can get another couple of nights away from their wives on company expenses. Assuming a lazy copy editor lets your comments through, you will be ostracised for eternity by the manufacturer in question, hunted to the ends of the earth, brutalised by trained monkeys and left to man a charity box in a shopping mall. They're *that* powerful.

Actually, they're not that powerful and that's all a bit of an exaggeration, but what they will do is immediately drop all advertising from your magazine or newspaper – including all affiliated car-manufacturer advertising, because they all own each other and there are, like, only two unrelated car companies left – causing you to be fired or your publication to go under, so that you will be out of a job, your ex-colleagues will ostracise you and you will end up manning a charity box in a shopping mall. So almost as bad, just no monkeys.

Don't believe me? Try finding a list of the Ugliest Cars On The

Road in any current publication. Specifically, look for a list of new cars that you recognise and may even spot in traffic. Chances are you won't come closer than a collection of obscure and probably obsolete models, mostly from Eastern Europe circa 1970 that you've hardly ever seen and possibly never heard of. The Skoda Estelle, anyone? The AMC Pacer? The Yugo GV?

That's because magazines and newspapers are too chicken to say, "Geez Ford people, what the hell were your designers shooting up when they came up with the Ka?" (A name that is missing a second "k", I'd suggest.) Or, "Hey BMW, your vehicle aesthetics are a big in-joke, aren't they?"

Luckily, this book receives no income whatsoever from automotive advertising – ha! – so, in the interest of setting the record straight, and given that we're not expecting a motoring sponsorship any time soon, here is what the current list of top ten ugliest cars on the South African road should look like.

1. Ford Ka. To prevent any further decline in public self-respect, only the blind should be legally allowed to drive the Ka(k) – although this strategy would likely provide health challenges of its own.
2. BMW 7 Series. Added proof that money can't buy taste.
3. Renault Kangoo. "It's very simple" is this car's tag line. They went with that instead of "It's very hideous".
4. Mahindra Bolero. Mahindra: not just cheap, unsightly too.
5. Fiat Multipla. They may have given it a face-lift, but you can face-lift Kathy Bates and she still won't be a beauty queen.
6. Dodge Nitro. Ugly on steroids.
7. Chrysler PT Cruiser. You either "get" this car's look, or you are normal.
8. BMW 1 Series. A brave attempt to match the horror of the 7 Series. Not quite but close.
9. Daihatsu Materia. Small and unattractive. The Verne Troyer of the road.

10. Toyota Prius. Proving that the environmentalists will never win because they haven't worked out that you can't change the world with ugly.

Interest rates
If only "interest rates" were just a measure of the rate of interest in a particular subject or phenomenon. Rather than the measure of acute pain and suffering you feel when you check your monthly bank statement and realise your car is now costing you as much as your house did a year or two ago, and that you might just be able to afford a 20kg bag of Vet's Choice to feed the family for the month once the bond payment goes through.

IT-support dorks
Once upon a time, in the technologically backward 1980s, the word "computer" conjured up astounding images of science fiction, of great human endeavour, of a highly intelligent, sophisticated future. Anyone remotely involved with this new science was a default genius, a prophet from cyberspace with a unique insight into a world the rest of us could only dream of. Unfortunately, this prophet is now called Malcolm, and he mans your internet service provider helpline from 9am to 5pm weekdays, excluding public holidays. Nothing quite warrants the phrase "fuck fuckity fuckfuck" like the realisation that you have to phone Malcolm for advice.

As the world gets smaller and smaller, and advanced computer technologies spread their influence through every aspect of our lives, as communications speed up exponentially and we are inundated with ever-more stupendous gadgets and gizmos, we are faced with the rise of the IT-support dork – who happens to think he's a cybergod when he is, in fact, just a glorified postal worker for the 21st century, and whose disdainful incompetence dressed up as preoccupied arrogance is enough to make you want to crush his balls out of frustration. Or even your balls if it means you can avoid having to talk to him.

If there is actually a cybergod out there, perhaps he'd be kind enough to deliver a message from me to the world's IT-support dorks. Something along the lines of, You are not a cyber god, IT support dork. You are a computer geek who used to get beaten up when you were a teenager, so lose the too-cool-for-school attitude and answer your support phone when I call. And make a little effort when you do; just because you can do some programming doesn't mean you can talk to me like I'm a pensioner asking for directions to the old-age home. I haven't shat in my pants and I don't give contemptuous sighs when you try to write something or communicate in English or pick up women, so cut me a break when I ask you why my computer is on fire. And maybe keep up to date with the product you're advising on, so you can actually be of some ready assistance. Then you'll be able to stop beginning the answer to every one of my queries by saying it's impossible and then saying maybe there's a way and then hitting two buttons, solving the problem and acting like you've just split the atom.

Jet Skis

Leaf blowers for the dam. (See **Leaf blowers**, *Kak 1*.)

Joburg architecture

Joburg has always been a den of flashy wealth and, as a result, it's always been rather ugly. Visual indigestion was par for the course on the Rand long before the advent of "Boere Baroque". But there have always been areas of resplendent, or at least cutting-edge, architecture to make up for it: the classic (if predictable) colonial buildings in the CBD; the fine houses in among the Hyde Park and Westcliff greenery; even the zooty high-rises in Sandton used to, on some levels, be bearable to look at.

Lately, though, things have taken a turn for the even worse, and the nouveau spread of appalling architecture appears unstoppable. On every street corner lies a pile of bricks next to yet another debacle-under-construction. Sandton, for one, is now littered with hi-tech eyesores that appear to be thrown together in a matter of weeks. Turn your back for a minute and suddenly there's another horror of modular glass and slate to frighten the bejesus out of you. Then pop down to Benmore to witness a pair of egregious apartment blocks going up, or cruise through Douglasdale or

Sunninghill for some quite disturbing suburban nightmares.

The nadir of early 21st-century Johannesburgia, however, seems to have congregated in the area between Coronation Road and Oxford Avenue in Sandhurst, a positively shock-and-awe-striking neighbourhood where resounding bad taste meets ludicrous bank balances. Whether it's a hideous chicken-shit faux-Tuscan McMansion with separate suitably imposing four-storey entrance and exit gates, or a pseudo-eclectic modernist regurgitation propped up by Corinthian columns and surrounded by a platoon of armed guards in camo fatigues, it seems there is no stopping the insanity of it all. If you had to make a call, Coronation is probably not quite as transcendentally horrendous as Oxford just yet – but that's like calling Ashlee the classy Simpson sister. Oh how the old money in the area must despair. They can, at least, be grateful for their 20-foot walls.

KFC advertisers' humour inconsistency

What's wrong with you people who do the TV commercials for KFC? One minute you're appalling, the next you're brilliant – then you're appalling again. You're like JP Pietersen on the rugby field. Or Halle Berry's choice in scripts. (*Swordfish* – *Monster's Ball* – *Catwoman…* Stop messing with our heads, Halle!)

First came the "Friends" campaign. Lest anyone's forgotten – or perhaps repressed the memory – this was the series of mortifying TV advertisements that featured Nick Boraine and Casey B Dolan pretending they were like the characters on *Friends*. Let's be clear on just how bad these ads were: very, very bad. (See **The KFC "Friends" Campaign**, *Kak 1*.)

But then came the wheel-changing ad where the chicken-drumstick-munching guy comes to the assistance of the woman who needs her tyre changed. Well acted, genuinely funny. Nothing like a bit of sexism to tickle the funny bone. Kudos all round.

But this was followed by the irritating girl ordering food with her boyfriend's mother, and then the other irritating girl ordering food with her boyfriend. "I'll have a twister, please…" How to put into words just how bothersome these ads were? Well, it's impossible really, but very, very, very is a good start.

What's the deal, KFC advertisers? Are you flipping a coin that has "witty and entertaining" on one side and "hell's commercials" on the other? Or is there a really sad case in your office called Neville who keeps coming up with ideas that you can't say no to because you're worried he's going to go home and gas himself if he's rejected one more time?

Stop playing with our emotions, please, and just fire Nev. He's not your responsibility.

KP – also known as Ego, also known as FIGJAM*, also known as Kevin Pietersen

There was, briefly, a time when we may have entertained the notion of just ignoring Kevin Pietersen; when we may have quietly contemplated the idea of bracketing him away with the begrudgingly respected Matthew Haydens and Ricky Pontings of the cricketing world – because the effort of loathing him was beginning to get a little bit tedious. But then they went and made him captain of England, which means he's inherited the mantle of that other gormless cricketing twat, Michael Vaughan. So we are now morally bound to loathe him, come what may. Well, at least it's not hard.

* Fuck I'm Good, Just Ask Me

Vernon Koekemoer

I fink he are a nice guy. But I also fink da media likes to make da celebrities for no reason. And anyway, Chuck Norris would hit him wif a one hand and make him feel like he are surrounded.

Kulula jokes

I laughed at one of them once. About six years ago.

L

Large car-insurance companies

Here's a neat trick. Try this next time you're bored and feel like saving R45 a month. Assuming you own a 1988 Golf II GTi.

First, phone up the large car-insurance company that you've been using for the last ten years and tell them to drop your monthly premiums – just for the hell of it. The guy on the end of the line will then tell you to take a hike. Politely, of course, but that will be his gist. He might just shave off three or four bucks to show that they care, though "there's absolutely no way we can go lower than that".

Next, call up another large car-insurance company, tell them what your premiums are and ask them if they can beat that. They will, by about R50. Tell them you'll think about it.

Now, phone up your large car-insurance company again – don't worry, you won't get through to the same agent – and tell them you've been given a quote of R50 less than you're currently paying by another large car insurance company. (If you want, you can skip the other stuff and start here, but where's the fun in that?) The agent will sound a trifle concerned, pretend to do a complicated mathematical sum on his computer, and offer you about R45 less than you're currently paying.*

The moral of the story: large insurance companies are bloodsucking hounds that would be happy to take food out of your mouth unless you keep them on a tight leash. They're run by soulless bean counters who work out every insurance contingency known to mankind to the nearest cent: hence the second company knows that you couldn't be bothered to jump ship for anything less than R50 a month and the first one knows it doesn't quite have to match that to keep you – the extra R5 is not worth the las for you. But it all adds up for them.

To be honest, my moral is a huge generalisation, but the tactics sure worked on Outsurance…

* See? In two months this book pays for itself!

Living in hope

Never before has a nation had so much potential. It's all around us! As the country goes about its daily grind of poverty, upping that HIV count and developing ever more creative ideas for molesting young children, we are consoled by a simple message that radiates out from inspired politicians and clever copywriters everywhere. "Hope." That's what we've got. Never mind electricity, employment or crime-free streets. Hope. I feel much better already.

As former PAC president Clarence Makwetu recently said after a four-hour emergency meeting to resolve the imminent collapse of his party, "Nothing has been concluded, but we have hope."

A pithy summary of the African condition, that line. Well, guess it's better than nothing. Though we shouldn't get so down on ourselves. We don't only have hope. We've got soap too. And, more importantly, dope. And the Pope.

Okay, not the Pope.

Load shedding – also known as another Eskom cockup

Remember when load shedding was a major aggravation that we had to put up with on an almost-daily basis? Man, did that chafe after a while. Then all of a sudden the rolling blackouts just stopped.

Rather interestingly it turns out our power-generating capacity didn't have all that much to do with those weekly sessions of sitting in the dark. Certainly we are running a bit short on power stations these days, but it seems the crisis in early 2008 was mostly due to coal stockpile problems – which boils down to bad administration.

There are a litany of charges of mismanagement lined up against Eskom – diverting power to Zimbabwe during the crisis, investing funds earmarked for power stations elsewhere to falsely boost financial results and so on – but let's just focus on the coal stockpiles. That is, Eskom couldn't work out that an adequate supply of fuel was required to create electricity without having to resort to load shedding. Not to be a stickler or anything, but how did the people in charge get their jobs?

Amazingly, the Eskom bigwigs saw fit to issue themselves with R10 million in bonuses in March 2008. No keeping a low profile and letting the storm pass for these guys: bonuses and new Mercs all around! And public enterprises minister Alec Erwin justified this astounding decision by noting that the books looked good. "They had done well in the past financial year," he said at the time. Dear Alec obviously needed things spelt out to him in his old age. Alec, in simple language: THE FIGURES LOOKED GOOD BECAUSE THEY SAVED MONEY BY LETTING EVERYTHING GO TO SHIT! They cut expenditure by not buying coal and by letting the country's power-generating infrastructure fall apart. That is not worthy of a bonus. That is worthy of radical disciplinary action and an overhauling of the entire power utility. You fool!

Alec may be gone now, but it's about time all the Eskom honchos who did their accounting classes at Enron or Fidentia followed suit – and if they would be so kind as to return their bonuses, which could go towards making up the $50 billion in direct losses that the power crisis is estimated to have cost the country. Then they could perhaps take up volunteer fire-fighting positions at their nearest substations, which are no doubt due for spontaneous combustion any day soon.

Local celebs

Joost and Amor, Jeannie D, Uyanda Mbuli, Khanyi Mbau, Edith Venter, Ursula Stapelfeldt, Vanessa Carrera, Claudia Henkel, Nicole Fox, Michael Mol, Dieter Voigt, Izak Strauss, Pam Andrews, Mags van der Westhuizen… Is this the best we can do? I don't even know who half these people are!

Oh Jesus, there's Danny K.

Low G.I. muffins

Low in G.I., low in flavour, low in desirability.

Lurking poo snakes

It's bad enough that you have to brave the indignity of making use of a public lavatory, which has been sat on by several hundred thousand people you don't know – many of them in the very long time since the seat last saw a trace of Toilet Duck squirted its way, and some of whom quite possibly suffer from highly contagious bum diseases – but then you are very often forced to suffer the added humiliation of contending with an unflushed bowl.

Even as you're closing the stall door behind you, you can tell you're doomed. No toilet paper, seat down: it's got non-flusher written all over it. You peer grimly over the bowl and there it is waiting for you: a foot-long brown mamba marinating in apple juice and waiting to strike…

Look, it's not polite to do this at home either, but exposing your special brand of chocolate milkshake to someone you don't know is just wrong. If you must let your yellow mellow, well then, okay, but – come on, people! – when it's brown flush it down.

Macon

I'm all for freedom of thought, which technically makes me all for freedom of religion. But when that freedom of religion impinges on my freedom to eat bacon then I start getting all conflicted. Macon is not the same! Sorry, Debonairs Halaal in Plumstead, not ordering from you again…

Madiba abuse

Please, for the love of all that is good in this land, can people stop using Nelson Mandela's name for personal and commercial gain? The man is quite literally our last steadfast point of integrity and decency, and every time a foreign celeb rocks up to have a picture taken with him, or a businessman names a diamond the "Madiba Diamond" as a publicity stunt for his new investment-management company, or someone tacks together a crappy sports magazine that looks like *Die Son* "in celebration of Madiba's 90th birthday", they're just taking advantage of his good name and trivialising his deeds. And making themselves look like money-grubbing pieces of shit.

Julius Malema and the ANC Youth League

Previously, no-one took the ANC Youth League seriously. Their last president, Fikile Mbalula, was still in power at age 36 – so it's not beyond the realm of possibility that the man was a grandfather at the time. He'd do something stupid and people would think, What's a guy in his fifties know about the kids of today anyway? And he'd say something stupid and people would think, Well he's, like 65 or something, he's going to forget his words every now and then. But now that Fikile has moved on to higher things, to a position on the NEC – where, unfortunately, people may take him seriously, Lord help us – let's see where that leaves us... Oh dear, that would be with Julius Malema.

When the ANC Youth League was started in 1944, it had the likes of Oliver Tambo, Walter Sisulu and Nelson Mandela at the helm: impressive, intelligent young men who would go on to rule the ANC and, in Mandela's case, the country. Now they have Malema in charge: an ill-advised militant troublemaker who will seemingly go on to be an ill-advised militant troublemaker for time eternal. And one who is particularly adept at making unconsidered, irresponsible and downright idiotic public comments. Considering the verbal dross the man generates, it seems logical to speculate that he suffers from one or more mental retardations. Particularly the one that makes sufferers believe they live on another planet.

Reports vary about the extent of Malema's education. Some say he doesn't have a matric; others say he finally scraped through (without exemption) at the age of 21. Either way, education – generally something people want in a leader – did not seem to be this guy's priority. Fighting the revolution was. He was politically active before he was ten, and by the time Mandela was leading South Africa in its first year as a newly liberated democracy he was learning how to fire guns and make petrol bombs. Which is to say, the reason for his military training had already passed and yet there he was, still training...

See where this is going?

In short, Malema is a redundant liberation fighter brought up to thrive in a political landscape that doesn't exist any more, and whose every political action is a justification for his existence.*

Earth to Julius, Earth to Julius. Come in Julius. In case you haven't heard, the revolution is over...

Of course, our chubby-faced rocket scientist is not picking up our – or anyone's – signal, and he hasn't been for a while, as is evident from a personal history replete with controversy. No-one who knew of his past would have been surprised to hear of his now-notorious "kill" comments in June 2008: "Let us make it clear now: we are prepared to die for Zuma. Not only that, we are prepared to take up arms and kill for Zuma" – which were later followed by league members chanting "Shoot to kill".

Of course, Malema tried the bog-standard out-of-context dismissal of the quote. "Don't impose liberal language [on us]," he declared. "We are using this [word] 'kill' to determine our passion and love in defence of the revolution."

Sorry, Julius, but that's the biggest lie since *The Neverending Story* and anyone with – let's see – a matric could work that out. The "take up arms" and "shoot to kill" bits kind of gave it away. And the later "elimination" talk wasn't fooling anyone, either.

Besides, how on earth does he expect his followers – many with similar training to him, many with similarly poor education, many who think that getting drunk and showing their arses is appropriate behaviour at a national conference – will interpret these words? Are they thinking, "Ah, our good comrade Julius is imploring us to kill for our leader Jacob. Of course by kill he is speaking in metaphors and encouraging us simply to act with passion and love. Because passion and love are so closely associated with killing"?

Or are they thinking that violence and, if necessary, killing is still an acceptable political tool? And perhaps a life tool too? (See **Violence as a kneejerk reaction**.)

One thing's for sure: we don't need a loud-mouthed militant in charge of an impressionable youth group, encouraging the quick-fix solution of thuggery and bloodshed whenever they want to get their way. What we do need is a bit of school time, some critical thinking and a general furthering of the notion that simply following around the kak-stirrer making the most noise is not the wisest option.

Here's to the return of common sense and rationality, and the continued decline in ANCYL membership and activity around the country. Julius, may you soon be presiding over but a small kindergarten class of hooligans...

* Political commentator Rebekah Kendal sums up Malema's upbringing as succinctly as anyone: "Like all child soldiers, he was indoctrinated with a default system of revenge, resolution through violence and paranoia of the unseen enemy. He was indoctrinated without any true capacity for understanding; without any objective points of reference; and without the emotional maturity to appreciate that sometimes forgiveness is more powerful than revenge." Thanks, Rebekah.

Marine Parade, Durban
Hobos, robbers, rapists and drunks. Beautiful.

Meddling sports administrators
It's not just South Africans who have to put up with a bunch of out-of-touch old farts looking out for themselves being put in charge of sports.

Just think of IOC president Jacques Rogge criticising Usain Bolt, the man who won three sprint gold medals in world-record breaking time at the 2008 Olympics, for daring to celebrate and play up to the crowds afterwards. Rogge didn't like the fact that Bolt didn't immediately congratulate his competitors. Never mind that the guy had just broken the world record and rewritten several laws of physics in the process, and was, by the time his competitors crossed the finish line, on the other side of the stadium. Or the fact that Bolt comes across as a genuinely nice guy who just likes to have fun (and redefine his sport).

Shut up and get in touch with the real world, you silly old man.

That said, you don't get worse than our lot. There's our hopeless South African Sports Confederation and Olympic Committee bunch who can barely hold clipboards from the sound of things, let alone organise foreign logistics or a vaguely respectable Olympic outfit. Why bother investing in our athletes when you can blow R11 million on a showcase for 2010 in a Beijing hotel that no-one attends? And the tact: business-class seats for SASCOC officials while Paralympic athletes get put in economy. Nice.

A level above this lot, though, is the Parliamentary Portfolio Committee On Sport And Recreation, run by Butana Khompela and Cedric Frolick, whose sole skills seem to be the ability to intervene in matters they know very little about, making a mockery of their sporting knowledge in the process.

Here is Pieter de Villiers being philosophical after one such incident: "I was appointed to make rugby decisions… We never said it was going to be a perfect world. If you look at the Bible, Joseph started out in the pit and ended up in the palace. There was a moerse lot of kak in between." It's a little out of context, but you catch his drift.

Medical-aid schemes

Scheme *n.*

1 a systematic plan for a course of action

2 a secret and cunning plan, especially one designed to cause damage or harm

All you want from your medical aid is to know that when the shit goes down and you grow a third nipple or your penis falls off, the medical bills will be covered. Instead, you get an annual Bible-thick review of the industry filled with impenetrable jargon and acronyms, each more complicated and mind-numbing than the last. MSA, CIB, CDA, ATB, SPG, CBP – WTF*? It's impossible to work out exactly what it all means but the bottom line is something along the lines of "We'll do whatever we can not to help you out in your time of need. If you're lucky we'll cover half the cost." That's my understanding of it, at any rate.

* Respectively: medical savings account, chronic illness benefit, chronic drug amount, above threshold benefit, self-payment gap, clawback period – what the fuck?

Morons

Just like idiots (see **Idiots**, *Kak 1*) – forwarding email hoaxes, listening to lippy unfunny DJs, watching MTV, watching *Clipz*, blogging, responding to blogs, getting offensive in chat rooms, crabbing through shopping malls, using car-engine ring tones, living off fast-food and wondering why they have diabetes, thinking the *Spider-Man* trilogy was great, waiting until they're right in front of the ATM to get out their wallets when they've been standing in the queue for five minutes already... and generally making life unbearable.

Mr Delivery

Slow, cold and shit.

Robert Mugabe

I have a theory. One day a long time ago, back when the Struggle still actually existed, Uncle Bob walked in on Thabo giving Manto a good old-fashioned seeing to. Thabo – caught between a cock and a dark place, as it were – was naturally somewhat embarrassed by the situation but swore both Bob and Manto to eternal secrecy. They agreed, on condition that Thabo would refrain from nagging about any misdemeanours, fashion faux pas and/or crimes to humanity that either of them may or may not commit in the decades ahead. On top of this, the recurring memory of Manto on the job slowly drove Bob insane. *Et voilà!* Three profound mysteries of our times solved in one go.

This theory is, of course, unproven, but I think you'll find it all adds up.

That multitonal alarm

You know the one. Bee-baw bee-baw, wowowowowowowow, aah aah aah aah, deedeedeedeedeedeedeedeedeedee, bee-baw bee-baw, wowowowowowowow, aah aah aah aah...

How does a person get away with inventing something like this without having liquid cement injected up his bottom?

Andy Murray

The next Tim Henman. Except better. And more of a knob.

Oh Jesus.

N

Neotel's introductory TV ad

Finally, after so many false starts, our second telecommunications company has arrived. Hallelujah, praise the Lord! The time of reckoning has come for Telkom and all in the land can rejoice. Although, let's be realistic, Neotel will probably turn out to be just another big fat incompetent telecommunications company (bad sign: its shareholders include Eskom and Transnet). And in the meantime, it could have made a far more memorable entrance. That commercial with all the little sign men running around was a nice concept and all, but it was way too understated. Considering it was the first time the South African public was being exposed to the brand, they really could have made their point a lot clearer. The obvious – and far cheaper option – would have been to film a guy holding up a sign that read "Up yours, Telkom".

Then they could have expanded the campaign with increasingly sophisticated slogans:

"'Telkom is bad. We are not Telkom."

"Let the evil be cast from your lives: come to Neotel."

"Telkom se poes. Brought to you by Neotel."

Tell me this wouldn't have had customers knocking down their door?

The never-ending celebrity-chef phenomenon

Lisping scooter queen Jamie Oliver isn't even the worst of them. If a guy is born with inherent antisocial behavioural problems, he becomes a chef so that he can shout at people. If he doesn't have his ingredients neatly pre-measured into precious little glass bowls, he has a row of herbs growing in pots from which he rips bunches of leaves to fling into his consommé, or his jus, or some other thing that basically means "sauce". Watch him chip-chop the cucumber like a ninja in a pouffy white hat. See him flamboyantly toss bits of badger flesh around in a pan. Hear him explain, "And we're going to keep the seasoning simple, to really bring out the flavour of the meat," casually splitting an infinitive and adding 12 simple spices plus the simple liver juice of four breeds of quail. Then he'll fashion a small tower on a big plate, take a bite and report to the camera, "Mmm… Delicious!"

And if he's not on my television set – I'm watching BBC Lifestyle, for crying in a bucket! Is there nothing else on? – he's at my table in the restaurant. Now, instead of your food appearing through the kitchen swing doors for you to eat, the chef comes too, taking it upon himself to share the secret of his special jus (translate: sauce) with you while his hands perform a spastic little dance in slow motion and you're expected to gaze at your plate with misty eyes. Shut up! I'm hungry, I want to eat! Go and speak to that table of old ladies over there. I'm sure they'll love the attention.

While restaurant names have all but disappeared in some circles, with people whispering in wonderment about the chef as if he *is* the restaurant, some of us still prefer our food without the melodrama, thanks very much. I'm a fan of the guy in the restaurant down the road from me. His name's Lennox and he makes a fantastic toasted egg-and-bacon sandwich – without any fuss. Anyone want to give him a show?

New Zealand and Australian rugby commentators' – and now South African rugby writers' – annoying habit of referring to South Africa as "the Republic"

Self-explanatory title.

"Next week on…"

You've just finished another titillating and thought-provoking episode of *The Tudors* and before you've even had a chance to let your heartbeat return to normal they're already telling you what's going to happen next week. This desperate strategy, now used on virtually every show on TV, was clearly devised to ensure that the interest of fickle viewers is piqued to such an extent that they wouldn't dare think of missing the next instalment. "Oh my, it looked like King Henry was about to make passionate love to a buxom courtier! Could it be? I'll just have to watch next week, I couldn't live with not knowing" seems to be the general reaction they're looking for.

Some advice for *The Tudors* viewers: King Henry makes passionate love to a buxom courtier every week. The trailers try to make it look exciting but it's actually rather dull. Just catch "Next week on…" and "Previously on…" and you can follow what's going on without having to watch the show.

And some advice for *The Tudors* producers: instead of creating action-packed trailers for every episode, rather save up the money and invent a time machine. Then go back to the 16th century and tell Henry VIII to stop being such a pussy and to fight a few wars. Your show would be much more exciting.

Nintendo Wii as a means of exercise

Look, everyone! It's my Wii! Anyone for tennis? It's awesome! We can play it right here in the living room!

A study by the *British Medical Journal* released in December

2007 found that children who played "active" games on consoles such as the Nintendo Wii used about two per cent more energy than those playing normal "inactive" consoles. That's correct: two per cent.

"These increases [are] of insufficient intensity to contribute towards recommendations for children's daily exercise," the authors of the study concluded. "As a result, little Freddy Fatboy is going to have to haul his ass outside and run around a bit if he wants to avoid growing up to be the Oros Man. We've also found that anyone who thinks that playing tennis in front of a TV screen is the equivalent of playing real tennis, which often involves actual running around, is not very clever. And the people in the Wii ads are way too bouncy and keen-looking. There should be more fatties to make it more plausible."

To be honest, they didn't really say that last bit, but I bet they wanted to.

Noise pollution

Shut up! Just shut the hell up! All of you!

Non-voters

Whining about politics in this country – and most countries, actually – is a national pastime. But you need to earn the moral high ground. No vote, no whine. *Comprende?*

The nouveau Cape bushveld experience

"Welcome to Mumbojumbo Private Game Farm. We are ever so sure that you'll enjoy your authentic big-five game-drive experience with us today. Note, please, the natural beauty of this recently converted sheep farm, which looks nothing at all like the African bushveld. Note also your first sighting of the day, to the left, an ostrich. Amazing. Unless you've seen a million of them before. And there on the right you should be able to make out our pair of Cape buffalo in the distance up against the fence, just over from the lonely-looking elephant. The elephant is the world's largest land animal. There should be another one around here somewhere. Coming up at the feeding trough is our recently imported white rhinoceros, which will have a mate arriving soon. Any day now. We're all really excited about that. Now, let's go visit the boma where we'll find the circus lions. Grrrr! They are still acclimatising and are due to be integrated with the other animals some time in the next 15 years. Then we'll head over to the model African village for a patronising 'traditional' tribal dance, and after that, the highlight of the day, lunch at the dining and conference area where we offer you a lousy buffet with overpriced drinks and your last sighting, a horde of common or garden-variety German tourists. If you're wondering about the leopard, forget it. There's one around here somewhere but no-one's seen it since 1996..."

Not quite Kruger. Not quite the zoo.

The NP revival

Here's some mildly disturbing news: the National Party is back. This is not to say that the New National Party is back because the New National Party – which is what the old National Party decided to call itself when it was trying to become respectable – isn't really what the new guys in charge have in mind. The New National Party was about trying very hard to cling to any last vestige of power in the '90s, whereas the new National Party is, as far as I can work out, about cashing in on white people's fears, promising satisfying public executions as often as possible and banning witches. Whatever it is or turns out to be, the National Party has registered with the Independent Electoral Commission to contest the 2009 elections. Curiously, Juan-Duval Uys, the former spokesman for "controversial" NPP leader Badih Chaaban (that must look good on the CV), who apparently did the registering along with a couple of ex-ID councillors, has declared that the party will be inclusive and non-racist. So why then is he calling it the National Party, which based its core policy on being exclusive and racist?

Remember apartheid, Juan-Duval? That was the NP's baby.

Numbers instead of words

Yes, *2Kak 2Furious* is ironic. In fact, if I must, drum roll please, it is just 2 ironic 4 words....

One-headlight drivers

So there you are cruising up the West Coast late of a Friday evening on your way out of town for some weekend relaxation and you figure you'll just pop past the overloaded bakkie with 12 guys in the back doing 40km/h in front of you because the only thing coming your way is a motorbike, or is that a bicycle with a particularly strong headlamp, and – holy shit! – it's a car with one light out and not just any car it's a great big motherfucking 1986 Mercedes 300SL, beige of course, that weighs as much as an M1 Abrams main battle tank, and you know the driver has one hand on the wheel and the other arm draped across the passenger seat and he's thinking "I brake for no-one" a) because that's just his vibe and b) because his car has the stopping distance of the *Exxon Valdez* which means he starts slowing down at Milnerton if he wants to stop in Woodstock although perhaps a swerve of sorts would be nice but that's not happening either, so you wrench your car back onto your side of the road and the bakkie veers onto the gravel behind you, kicking up stones and flinging passengers into the night, while your car slides all over the place and you realise you've just wet yourself, and later that night you cry yourself to sleep.

For some reason, South African drivers just don't realise that setting out with only one working headlight at night leads to a high proportion of near-death life-scarring experiences. Fix your lights, please. Or at least swerve a bit.

Opening ceremonies

Meh. Where's the sport? If I ever want to spend three hours watching a visual extravaganza with people running around in "national dress" doing choreographed tumble rolls with some colourful lights zooting around in the background, well, then I'll know that my life has become inordinately sad and it's time to put and end to the futility of it all. I'm thinking I'll overdose on Viagra and go out with a smile on my face.

I suppose the opening ceremony in Beijing was pretty good, from the five minutes I saw. Digitally added fireworks aside. (And civil oppression blah blah blah…) But then we had to sit through that first week of Olympics. What a mind-numbing exercise in boredom that was. Personally, I think the spectators would have had far more fun dropping acid and looking at Chinese air pollution until the athletics began. And they'd have lost fewer brain cells in the process.

They say that if a sport is in the Olympics then it must matter. And to this I counter, what about handball? For God's sake. How do you compare an athlete who runs the 100m in less than 9.7 seconds and then the 200m in 19.3 seconds with a bunch of palookas running around playing handball? Yes yes, I'm sure it's harder than it looks, but so is morris dancing. Then there's judo, air pistol, softball, badminton, dressage, BMX racing… Yawn. Honestly. What's next? Olympic pick-up sticks? Olympic on-on?

Someone could perhaps look into the Olympic soccer tournament too. Who deemed an under-23 tournament as the way to go? I'm thinking they wanted to get soccer at the games to attract viewers but FIFA wouldn't let them take full teams, what with there being a World Cup and all. So they went with players under the age of 23 so as to maintain a precedent set with… no Olympic sports. And three over-23s are allowed per squad. How arbitrary.

I say it's time to cull it down. The only sports people really want to watch are athletics, aquatics and gymnastics. And women's beach volleyball, naturally. So how about a back-to-basics Olympics where it's all about faster, higher, further? It would be sooooo much more interesting. And a lot cheaper too. Hell, Durban would even have a shot at hosting 2020.

Overpriced deli food that's nothing more than glorified Woolworths

Just add a hand-written label (or a hand-writing-font label) and make sure you don't vacuum pack your produce, and you're on your way to being a deli-food supplier. Then whack on an "organic" stamp if you want to up it to the next level.

Brilliant. Now you can mark up your chocolate cookies through the roof and charge R125 for a run-of-the-mill chicken-and-leek pie that may leave two people satisfied. If they've just eaten. And don't forget the olive oils. The more you charge, the better they think it is.

But seriously, why do people shop at Melissa's and then go back to shop there again? What am I missing?

Overpriced overhyped deconstructive cuisine

Would sir be interested in a sliver of kudu carpaccio paired with a triangle of Parmesan ice cream? A shot glass of truffle and diced ocelot flaked with lobster dust? *Soupçon* of froth with a teaspoon of fire/ice toothfish tartar foam? Microscopic warthog loin atop a bed of shaved haricot vert on a plate the size of Lesotho? Pre-dessert of unidentified aromatic textures served in test tubes on the bough of a tree? Implosion of dark-chocolate bonbon puddled with snail jus on a cheese grater? Lattice-work of Paraguayan coffee presented in a lamp shade?

No, sir would fucking not. Sir would like to know how the hell deconstructive restaurants have been charging such obscene prices, for soulless, unsatisfying and frankly stupid meals and getting away with it for so long. Alternatively, sir would like to know why deconstructive chefs, who fancy themselves "artists" with "visions", don't just drop their trousers, crack one off the wrist into a wine glass and serve that. Isn't that what it's all about?

P

Essop Pahad

"We need to understand that xenophobia has historically been used by right-wing populist movements to mobilise particularly the lumpenproletariat against minority groups in society."

Whatever, dude.

Who in the world can use the term "lumpenproletariat" without coming across as an obfuscating, aloof dickhead? Evidently not Essop Pahad.

Paper jams

Remember that '80s show we used to watch, *Beyond 2000*, with the nice Aussie narrators telling us about the almost incomprehensible wonders of the future that were in store for us? A personal computer that could fit in a brief case, a telephone that didn't require cables, a portable music player that could store several tape cassettes' worth of music. Wow, wow and wow! Pity they never said anything about the photocopier that can operate for more than five minutes without the goddamned paper jamming.

Here we are nearly a decade beyond 2000, with our iPhones and high-definition televisions and satellite navigation, and they still can't manufacture a freaking printer that doesn't break out in flashing orange lights 30 seconds into your 180-page print-out that you hoped would be done by the time you got back from dropping off the 11 o'clock monster. If it is actually a paper jam – because sometimes it isn't; sometimes the printer just likes to *pretend* it's a paper jam – you now have to dismantle the machine piece by piece and retrieve teeny bits of crumpled and torn paper from deep within its inner workings as if you're a brain surgeon – which, of course, you are not. (Note: brain surgeons *never* have to make photocopies.)

Amazingly, the inventor geeks have managed to come up with a printer called a stereolithograph that can create three-dimensional models of whatever it is you want to replicate (using smart polymers, FYI), but the normal reliable black-and-white copier is still seemingly beyond them. A galaxy of daily infuriation could be avoided by its invention. (Or, if it already exists, its delivery to our office. Thanks.)

Parents who insist on bringing their babies to public events

Hypothetical question: what will happen if a two-month-old baby attends a Starfinder course at his local planetarium? Hmmm.

Some possibilities:

1. It's going to struggle with the concept of sidereal versus solar time.
2. It won't be able to pronounce some of the longer star and constellation names. Triangulum Australe, Proxima Centauri, Betelgeuse and so on.
3. At some point it will start to cry and annoy everyone else in the room.

I'm almost certain on the first two, and I'm absolutely positive on the third.

Similarly, in a restaurant, two-month-old babies don't really appreciate the medium-rare Chateaubriand – and they cry. And in the cinema they don't often "get" the movie – and they cry.

Note the pattern here? Because their parents sure don't.

Parents who think their kids are the best in the world

Which is practically all of them.

Dear parents out there, I wouldn't want to upset you or anything, but you need to know this: your little darling is not the next Einstein. Yes, he's learnt how to write his name and that's just great. Truly. But it's on my living-room wall. In red crayon. And I'm not cool with that. And all his classmates are on to the 12-times table already anyway.

It's wonderful that you've managed to work out how to reproduce successfully but now it's time to calm down and get a little perspective. And maybe a hysterectomy.

Now take the crayon out of little Albert's nose.

Pee on the seat in the handicapped loo

What, are you retarded or something? Oh.

Pedestrians with a death wish

We've been here before, I know (see **Pedestrians**, *Kak 1*). All pedestrians are idiots. But our beloved minister of transport is not making any inroads into resolving the situation, so I feel obliged to offer a few more pointers to my fellow countrymen out there whose behaviour suggests that they are not just in the unlucky position of having to cross a six-lane highway but are actually trying their hardest to tackle speeding cars in the process.

Firstly, the cars will win. This is the score every time a two-ton chariot of doom takes on a 60kg pedestrian:

Two-ton chariot of doom   1

60kg pedestrian   0

Got that? It never changes. There's no Pedestrian Day. David and Goliath? For your purposes, they never met.

Secondly, if you're going to go, go. None of this stop-start now-I'm-going now-I'm-not business. You're going to give someone a heart attack one of these days and, just to prove a point, he's going to run you down with his dying breath.

And thirdly, having established that South African drivers are as aggressive, incompetent and inconsiderate as they come (see **South African drivers**, *Kak 1*), no amount of your "Ja, just go ahead and try" jaywalking telepathy is going to get the guy in the "330i boykie" or "You'll never walk alone Hi-Ace" to stop, slow down or effect the slightest collision-avoidance manouevres. So get the hell out of the way.

The petrol price

You drive past the local Shell, where they've taken to displaying the petrol price in large digital figures like a horrifying death-toll counter, and you think to yourself, What the hell, that can't be right, my eyes must be playing tricks on me because that insanely high number I just saw cannot be the petrol price, surely? So next time you drive past you make a point of checking and it turns out that number you saw is not the petrol price – it's now *higher* than what you saw. It's ridiculous! You can get a major service for the price of a tank of unleaded now.

Here's some gloomy reading – the price of a litre of premium petrol on the Reef over the last 25 years:

August 1983: R0.59
August 1988: R0.91
August 1993: R1.75
August 1998: R2.44
August 2003: R4.02
August 2008: R10.40

At least we don't live in Norway. It's close to R20 a litre there. And it's Norway.

Pizza-delivery boys

Dude, I used to deliver pizzas. I've been there. It's boring, you're tired, you brake too hard at a robot and the box with my pizza in it falls on the floor. It happens. But at least straighten the thing out before handing it over to me. Because in all probability I'm going to open the box. In which case I'm going to see that it's all over the place – chances of me missing it are pretty slim. And then I'm going to tell your manager to get medieval on your ass. *Stupidisimo!*

Please-call-me SMSes

There was a time when receiving a Please-call-me might have lent an element of prestige or at least respect to the receiver, with the implication that he was in some kind of emergency-work-related employment – a doctor or paramedic or something. The pager: what a handy little device that was. But now that we have cellular telephones it has largely been consigned to the technological scrapheap. If only the Please-call-me message, the defining icon of contemporary loser status, would follow suit. The cheek!

Portaloos

Inevitably it's the J&B Met or some other wannabe swanky outdoor public event when the brown dog decides he wants out and he wants out bad. He's scratching at the back door and you're short of options. So there you are – in the good shirt and chinos, no less – and you're sweating bullets in the late-afternoon sun waiting your turn at the double row of Portaloos. Scratch scratch. Scratch scratch. A couple of Breezer-buzzed teen slappers with their tits half out are falling all over themselves in front of you but you're not even interested because you've got a shit on your mind. A shit in a Portaloo. Jesus, the Portaloo.

Inside, it's a hot box. A day's worth of human bowel movement microwaved by the midsummer heat. You remember not to breathe, but you make the fool's mistake and hazard a peek. Oh. My. God. There aren't 50,000 individual turds down there any more, oh no – they've merged into one… *thing*, oozing and pulsating as if possessed of an insidious life force. It's Jabba the Hutt, man.

So now you're about to crap on something that's basically alive, but there's nothing else for it. You've unbuckled, without letting your pants touch the floor, and you're hovering – like the chicks always say they do – even though you've thrown down as much tatty one-ply as possible, and you're still trying desperately to hold your breath but the reek is penetrating your very pores, you can actually taste it, and now tears are rolling down your cheeks because it's just so degrading...

How they haven't made a B-grade movie titled *Night Of The Living Portaloo*, I don't know. Because it's a horror show in there. For the love of all things merciful, it's the 21st century. Is this the best we can do?

The preponderance of South African acronyms

So many of them! And so many of them are bloody annoying. ANCYL + COSATU + SAA + NP + SACP + SADP + POPCRU + NUMSA + SANCO = PAINFUL

Public protests that aren't really thought through particularly well

It's not just students complaining about tuition fees who break things when they want to attract attention to their plight (see **Violent student protests**, *Kak 1*). In August 2008, angry commuters in KwaMhlanga took it upon themselves to set ablaze 30 Putco buses, causing damage in the region of R20 million, after what appears to have been several days of difficulty organising tickets and fares.

"We were angry when the bus tickets were not sold. Some of us didn't go to work and Putco is unreliable and we don't have other means of transport," explained one Mandla Mthembu. He did not, however, go on to explain how destroying 30 buses was going to remedy the situation.

Unfortunately, this was not an isolated incident. There is certainly a lot to complain about in this country – and in the world in general – but let's work on those constructive, meaningful protests please, people.

Q

The Q7

How could you, Audi? How could you defile your good name with that beast wagon of a Q7, beloved vehicle of choice for Russian mafia-types and steroid junkies everywhere? Not only an unholy step into the realm of road-hogging SUV overcompensation but an unsightly one at that, as though they inflated an A4 with ugly juice and added some extra ugly towards the rear. Is there anyone anywhere with the barest modicum of taste who owns one? Or has even seen one in the street without recoiling in horror and clutching at his face in agony? I certainly doubt it. For shame!

The tremendous success of the second-generation A3 was perhaps the first omen that things were not all as they should be at Audi HQ. Evidently some of the Vorsprung gentlemen were unhappy with merely being the German car manufacturer of choice for discerning drivers around the world. They wanted the world! (Or at least mainland Europe.) So they came up with an accessible and excellent entry-level luxury car that sold like hot cakes to everyone who didn't want a 1-Series. Then they jazzed up their previously fantastic-looking TT, presumably with design assistance from Chrysler or Nissan, so that it suddenly appealed to estate agents and high-class hookers. And then, to this mix they added the Q7, a car that could well share a Friday-afternoon drink with a Dodge Nitro or even – oh, how this pains me – a Hummer. (See **Hummers**, *Kak 1*.)

It seems the Audi board decisions are not all unanimous at the moment – as evidenced by the fantastic looking A5, the remarkable R8 and the potentially bearable Q5 – but it's high time those traitorous members who have sold their souls (and possibly write *Grey's Anatomy* scripts in their spare time, see *Grey's Anatomy*) be excommunicated from Ingolstadt. Otherwise there may be no stopping the slippery slide into BMWness…

Queuing for popcorn

One of the greatest inventions of all time – comparable with PVR and even bacon – is online ticket booking. Now you don't have to arrive half an hour before the movie starts and suffer a 300-person queue filled with offensive teenaged delinquents, at the end of which is a surly Ster-Kinekor staffer who really should be more upset for you that the only seats still available are in row Z. Instead, you can breeze into the cinema during the trailers, run the credit card through the automatic ticket dispenser and head straight to your prime viewing position. Assuming you don't want popcorn, that is.

Because if you do want popcorn, well, it's the 300-person queue, just one floor up, complete with offensive delinquents and even surlier staff operating in extreme slow motion (like that camera they had at the Olympics) who don't seem to get that the movie started two minutes ago and some of us are in a hurry. And let's not forget the criminal prices. R35 for microwaved corn and flavoured soda water? Mid-evening robbery, that is!

So online ticket booking is only half the solution. What they need is an all-inclusive internet-order system. Swipe your card and the machine issues you with tickets, popcorn, coke and a zap gun for vapourising teenagers. Shweet.

Quiet diplomacy's standing as a theory that worked out in the end

"Nobody challenges that, after many years, for the first time, the opposition was able to freely canvass in the urban and rural areas," said Aziz Pahad in April 2008 in defence of Thabo Mbeki's quiet-diplomacy approach to dealing with Robert Mugabe and the socio-economic meltdown of Zimbabwe that had been going on since 2000. Which was a bit like saying that the British appeasement of Hitler in the 1930s worked. Certainly there was a bit of a bad patch – you know, the war and the Holocaust and 70 million dead – but by 1945 things were pretty much exactly where Neville Chamberlain would have wanted them. Except there wasn't even peace in Zimbabwe when arsehole Aziz saw fit to pronounce on the ultimate success of quiet diplomacy. Not by a long shot.

The breathtaking denial of Mbeki's diplomatic failure by die-hard Thabo supporters continued even as Mugabe refused to concede defeat on release of the results of the (relatively) free and fair March elections; and they continued as Bob and Thabo, old pals that they are, made a mockery of the ongoing crisis by holding hands in front of international media; and as the generals set about torturing and murdering opposition supporters in the lead-up to the subsequent "runoff" in June; and as Mugabe declared his intentions never to concede power. "We are not going to give up our country for a mere X on a ballot," he announced without worry of any comebacks. "How can a ballpoint pen fight with a gun?"

The runoff was, of course, boycotted by the MDC because no-one (read South Africa) bothered to do, or even say, anything about the widespread violence and intimidation. Responsibility for the subsequent illegal Zanu-PF victory and Mugabe's conniving return to a position of negotiating strength can thus be placed – lock, stock and barrel – at Thabo's quietly diplomatic feet. And yet the defence continues.

Compare Mugabe's bellicose talk with this typically Thaboesque comment from our softly spoken mediator, regarding the subsequent frequently stalled power-sharing talks: "I am certain that the millions of Zimbabweans… await with great high hopes a positive outcome from our deliberations." Really, Thabo? You're not thinking they wanted you just to prattle on like you have for the last eight years, leaving them to starve and suffer under 11 million per cent inflation? Or was it 111 million per cent inflation? How do you tell the difference?

Quiet hand-holding ultimately had nothing to do with Mugabe even thinking about cutting a deal with the MDC. The fact is his people voted against him, despite his and his generals' best efforts to prevent this happening. As much as he tried to avoid it, eventually there was no other option. That Thabo could never work this out, as he tried his best to negotiate a presidential legacy for himself, is the truly astounding thing. Not even a harsh word – let alone a decisive action – against a man responsible for the deaths of thousands, the starvation of his people, the downfall of Zimbabwe's economy and the influx of four million refugees into South Africa (with resulting catastrophic consequences down here). Perhaps one day, when Thabo realises his revered Uncle Bob was never likely to just disappear quietly into the background, he will also work out what Mugabe has obviously known from day one and what we all know now: that our quiet diplomat is a sad, misguided fool. It may also occur to him that if he had spent less time meddling ineffectively in the affairs of other countries and more time running his own, he would quite possibly not have been unceremoniously ejected from office before his expiry date. (See **Robert Mugabe**.)

R

Recipe speak
Take two scoops of unoriginality, a pinch of plagiarism and a dash of sick, and you have the recipe for the laziest kind of metaphor ever.

Restaurants that issue their cutlery wrapped in a serviette
Often secured with a large sticker emblazoned with the restaurant's name. Must it be so goddamned tight? And must the sticker be so goddamned large? By the time you've torn it to pieces trying to liberate your knife and fork, you may as well have a cotton bud left over to mop up the plate of burger sauce you will now invariably drop into your lap.

Roadworks
I'm happy that we make an effort to fix our roads, truly I am. The potholes certainly won't fill themselves in. But how long does it take to put in a highway lane? Does the N2 to Cape Town International un-build itself at night or what?

Cristiano Ronaldo's modern slavery, as per Sepp Blatter
In light of speculation in mid-2008 that Alex Ferguson would

refuse to release Cristiano Ronaldo for transfer to Real Madrid, FIFA president Sepp Blatter had this to say: "I think in football there's too much modern slavery in transferring players or buying players here and there, and putting them somewhere."

As poor greasy Cristiano commutes to Old Trafford in his Rolls-Royce to continue suffering the tyranny of Sir Alex's merciless abuse, he must feel a genuine sense of connection with the slaves who were shipped to the New World in squalor and deprivation two centuries ago. No doubt he sheds tears for Kunta Kinte every time he cashes his weekly £120,000 pay cheque.

Sometimes the heart pain is just so acute when the horrific working conditions of modern footballers comes to light.

Sepp Blatter. What a twat.

Robben Island

Once upon a time, Robben Island was a world-famous icon of our national heritage inexorably linked with our most famous and exceptional person, Nelson Mandela, and looked upon by South Africans with a sense of reverence and respect. Now it is a world-famous icon continually mired in controversy that appears to have been run into the ground by your common cartel of corrupt and/or inept South African officials. In the 2006/7 financial year the island – which, in case anyone's forgotten, is a tourist trap that should be raking in money hand over fist – sustained a loss of R25 million. Naturally, "financial irregularities" were discovered and the island's CEO, chief operating officer and chief finance officer suspended to face disciplinary action and possible criminal charges, pending the outcome of a forensic audit.

In the meantime, the Robben Island Museum council suffered the ignominy of having its brand-spanking-new ferry, the *Sikhululekile*, attached because of outstanding debts owed to the company that manufactured the boat. Sjoe. Bit embarrassing…

While this was all going on, no-one seemed to notice that the local vegetation was disappearing and scores of animals dropping down dead. By winter 2008, the island had been stripped clean mostly by fallow deer and thousands of alien rabbits, which then had to be culled or relocated to the mainland to revive the ecosystem and hopefully save the few remaining indigenous buck. And then, to top it all off, there was that slightly embarassing debacle about the sea bed between the island and the V&A Waterfront possibly being sold off to a consortium of foreign companies…

Robben Island is a World Heritage Site, for crying out loud! Someone, do something to sort it out! Or next thing we're going to discover it's being used as a testing ground for intercontinental ballistic missiles.

Robot hawkers

Take your pick from inferior-quality rugby shirts, black bags you can very nearly see through, cheap plastic hangers, knock-off cellphone chargers, pirated DVDs or kids' toys that won't last the drive home. Or just ease your guilt by buying a *Big Issue*. It's not bad, actually!

Rugby-website pun fun

South African rugby-website subs. Sure, they may not be copy-editing for *The Spectator* any time soon, but you'd be amazed at the ingenious thought processes required for them to come up with endless pun-ridden article headers on a regular basis. Since extensive marketing research revealed that the majority of South African rugby-website readers are dedicated aficionados of the art of punning as the highest form of wit and entertainment, this is pretty much all they do.*

The highlight of the year is surely the Super 14 competition, where our subs are known to consume vast quantities of inspiring beer while reporting on match after punnable match. Herewith, some genuine article headers:

"Bullish Bismarck should be fit" – for forthcoming Bulls game.
"Drotske won't feel too Blue" – for forthcoming Blues game.

"Stormers blow over Hurricanes". This one is particularly clever, due to the coincidental juxtaposition of two teams named after weather patterns that have then been interconnected with the verb "blow". Which is what a wind does. This header may well have taken several weeks for its creator to hone and you can be sure he was rewarded with several funnels as a result.

Of course, articles involving the Perth-based Western Force are perpetual favourites. "Mitch needs rein-Force-ments" is a noteworthy headline that quite possibly won a rugby-website award, and at the very least warranted the sub in question a double funnel. You might say he was on the ball with that one. Har-har! (Sorry.)

Here's a not-so-original one, used by at least one site whenever the Force win a game: "A Force to be reckoned with". No funnels there. Maybe just a shotgun.

Despite the wealth of possibilities that the Super 14 throws up, our quite remarkable headline artists are not inhibited during the rest of the year, as this work of quite staggering genius illustrates: "Wendell's 'sailing' back to league". That's a yard glass right there! Note the quote marks, so that 'slow' readers don't miss the hilarious and profound literary parallel between Wendell Sailor's surname and the manner in which he is returning to play league rugby.

And if these talented subs cannot sneak a pun into a header somehow – though you can be assured they will spend many hours, even days, pushing themselves to the limit to find one – they will ultimately defer to any of various figures of speech, such as parallel irony, metonymy, synesthesia and transferred epithet. Um, actually no. The best they can come up with is alliteration. Usually stupid alliteration, like this: "Michalak's magic is manifesting".

What that even means, I couldn't really say.

---

* The research also revealed that they're mental in the head, by the way. The readers that is. And the subs, come to think of it – if not before they started managing these sites, then at least after a couple of months on the job.

S

The SACP

Someone should think about telling Blade Nzimande and his fellow comrades at the South African Communist Party that Stalin is not a good role model. Nix.

Sandton City Shopping Centre

Even though the logical response to any suggestion, ever, to visit Sandton City should always be "I would rather set fire to my ass. That's where evil lives", sometimes you find yourself agreeing to pop along with your girlfriend. Why? Hard to say. Forgetfulness, perhaps. Or chick hypnotism.

It's a warzone just to get there, fighting your way through Gautrain-related detours, fibre-optics-cable-laying snarl-ups and general construction-site detritus. Then, when you've finally found parking on the far corner of the roof and you descend into the doom-laden air of Mordor, you realise that the streets of Sandton had nothing on this place. It's a pitched battle just to make your way to Totalsports, where you have more chance of finding Madeleine McCann than a competent salesman. Then wrestle your way over to Uzzi or Timberland for the concert-level hip-hop to blast you right back out into the sea of mindless shoppers, either charging about like rampaging Orcs or crabbing listlessly into your path. Out of my way, moron! (See **Morons**.) By the time you make it to @Home, the idea of investing in a couple of Wüsthof carving knives so you can cut a swathe out through Woolworths and back to the car is rather appealing. (They may also come in handy if your local hijackers decide to follow you home to relieve you of your purchases.)

Sandton City aside, why do people spend so much time in shopping centres? Fourways, Canal Walk, The Pavillion… What is it about a conglomeration of soulless, inward-facing, fluorescent-lit shops that says, "Come spend all day here. Give us all your money. Eat at one of our crappy fast-food joints. Take a dump in one of our toilets"?

Sequels

Highlander II must rate as one of the worst movies of all time – not far behind *Battlefield Earth* – because it took an awesome concept and murdered it. But actually that was the only shit sequel. Otherwise they're all great.

Ahem.

Service delivery

"What's that, sissie? You were promised a house 15 years ago? Ooh right, about that… See, that special offer ended in 1994. It was part of our 'win the masses campaign' – which stopped once we had won the masses."

Is anyone really surprised at the levels of crime in this country? How would you feel if someone had been promising you something for 14 years and not made good on any of it? Some tip-of-the-iceberg facts:

• Since 1994 the number of South Africans living on less than R10 a day has more than doubled. As of 2005, the figure was at 4.2 million, up from 1.9 million in 1996.

• In 2007, just more than ten per cent of the black population accounted for more than 50 per cent of all black buying power.

• By 2006 a quarter of the South African population lived in informal squatter camps, many without adequate services, and with a growing backlog of houses in all but two provinces.

Sheesh. It's enough to make you want to beat a foreigner.

The bottom line is that even if we had the most kickass police force in the world, with Batman roaming the streets of Hillbrow and a CSI team for every murder, together with the most efficient criminal-justice system ever created, we would still be inundated with crime. It's what happens when people get put on hold for a decade and a half.

And if anyone dares complain – so '90s! – one or other obstinate politician will start rolling out facts and figures from various obscure reports that show 15 schools have been built in the North West, 100 kilometres of water pipes have been laid in Garies and the road between Port St Johns and Lusikisiki has recently been tarred. You're then looked at with revolutionary scorn as if you are the agent of the devil for doubting the government's promises to deliver.

All this time, the millions of South Africans who are aren't educated enough to question their leaders*, because they didn't make it into one of those 15 schools, sit at home in their creaking shacks wondering where their next meal's coming from. And those without the patience to wait for a lousy cement-block two-roomed house in outer Germiston that may come their way in the next decade or so if they're lucky, figure it's just easier to liberate a BMW and live the life. Or there's the Lotto-on-wheels option: the cash-in-transit van. Nothing says "instant delivery" like R5 million pottering along the N1 and guarded by redundant prison wardens without the firepower to frighten off a bag-snatcher.

Meanwhile, back at the government palace, the word "delivery" generally refers to the delivery of an Ellerines Colorado three-piece leather lounge suite or a heavily discounted luxury German car.

* Many of whom who are equally badly educated it seems: it was revealed in August 2008 that as many as a third of South Africa's municipal councillors are illiterate and cannot understand budgets.

Schabir Shaik's definition of "prison"

In November 2006 Jacob Zuma's former "financial adviser" began his 15-year sentence for fraud and corruption; but he's spent most of his time in minimum-security hospital wards due to "stress-induced hypertension". In August 2008, Yunis and Moe Shaik appealled for his release on medical grounds, declaring that their brother's imprisonment was "turning into a virtual death sentence" and he "weally, weally doesn't want to stay in pwison". Actually, they didn't say that second bit, but they may as well have. Not to be too callous or anything, but YOU'RE NOT SUPPOSED TO ENJOY JAIL! IT'S NOT A HEALTH RESORT! MAYBE YOU SHOULDN'T HAVE DONE ALL THAT ILLEGAL STUFF IN THE FIRST PLACE!

Shitty timeshare-scheme presentations dressed up as opportunities to win great prizes

A smartly dressed woman approaches your girlfriend in a shopping mall parking lot and tells her she's won one of several prizes: possibly a flatscreen TV, possibly a sound system, possibly something else. All she has to do is pop in to a short presentation that evening, whereafter she can pick it up – no obligations. So she comes home and tells you about it and you're watching highlights channel and not really thinking but you hear the bit about winning a flatscreen and that sounds interesting so you agree to go along, and next thing you're walking into a cheap and depressing neon-lit boardroom with several other vaguely concerned-looking couples, regretting the fact that your sceptical nature doesn't override your curiosity more often. After a half-hour video presentation on a points-system-holiday setup that looks suspiciously like a lame timeshare scheme, a guy called Alviro sits you down at a plastic table to repeat the video presentation word for word then run you through a tatty brochure of what appears to be the widest range of affiliated three-star hotels and caravan parks in the southern hemisphere, whereafter he assures you that just R45,000 a year will guarantee you at least seven days at any of these fine establishments, availability notwithstanding, and holiday time is something to be appreciated, isn't it?

The defining beauty of the evening is not so much the unmitigated con of it all as much as Alviro's unbridled resentment when you tell him that timeshare isn't really your cup of tea, as if *you've* wasted *his* time. And it almost goes without saying that you don't get the sound system or the flatscreen and that "something else" turns out to be a free hand job from the local sumo wrestlers' association. Well, it may as well be.

Shorty
Perchance does anyone know to whom exactly this Shorty individual refers in all of the rap music?

The silent treatment
It never works, chicks. NEVER. It just makes us annoyed and stubborn. If you've got a problem, tell me about it, don't expect me to miracle it out of your furrowed brow. (But don't take this as licence to go on all night about whatever it is I've done to hurt your feelings.)

SMS spam
I receive a quite adequate amount of email spam at the moment that I am sure will tide me over for the foreseeable future, so if it's all the same to you I'd rather prefer not be on your SMS mailing list, thanks very much. Where did you get my number from, anyway?

Sportsmen who chew gum with their mouths open
Soccer managers do it, too, but mostly it's a cricketing thing. From

what I can work out, the Aussies started it, but now the Proteas have picked up on this particularly distasteful habit. Prime offender is one-day all-rounder Vernon Philander, who is frequently filmed facing incoming fast bowlers while masticating like a masticating cow on the masticatingest day of the year. Someone at Cricket South Africa needs to have a word with the boy. Alternatively, he can change his name to Vernon Philanderer and then I won't mind so much.

The Springboks

Debacle, debacle, debacle, win World Cup, celebrate for a day and a half, debacle, whiny book, debacle, debacle, debacle, win first game in New Zealand for ten years, debacle, debacle, debacle.

That's pretty much the last two years in a nutshell. Copy and paste for the last 15. And we're one of the two greatest rugby-playing nations on earth.

Sylvester Stallone's failure to realise that age really is an issue sometimes

Dude, you're 62. You should be fighting Alzheimer's, not world boxing champs and the Burmese army. And now there's talk there might be a fifth Rambo… Jesus, Sly, who're you trying to kid?

Stompie chuckers

In 1914, King Ferdinand of Bulgaria took delivery of his new customised four-cylinder Daimler. Being a keen smoker, he had had it installed with the world's first ashtray in a car, an act that in itself did not initiate the First World War, but you can bet everyone else thought he was a right extravagant bastard. Most cars didn't even have roofs back then and there he was with an on-board ashtray. Fancied himself, he did. If he wasn't the king you can bet there would've been a jealousy-induced road-rage incident involving a baseball bat somewhere along the line. Perhaps.

Eventually, though, people caught on to this ground-breaking feature of automotive engineering and it became the norm in all cars. Smokers used their on-board ashtrays as a receptacle for their ash and even their extinguished cigarettes. Over the decades, though, they became aware of the noxious in-car odours this resulted in and they took to emptying their ashtrays into road-side gutters and No-hot-ash public bins. Humans are prone to natural progression, so the next logical step was to keep the cigarette, smoke and ash out of the car entirely, while still enjoying the pleasures of smoking and driving, a progression that turned out to be something of a regression, with smokers reverting to what King Ferdinand must have done before he took delivery of his new car: hanging their arms out the sides of their cars and dropping ash and cigarettes in the street.

But times are a-changing again. In America, Chrysler has taken the bold step to remove ashtrays entirely from their cars – to be replaced by an extra cup-holder for their milkshakes (Americans: more into heart disease than lung cancer) – realising that the next generation of drivers think smoking has as much appeal as driving goggles. Unfortunately, being a little short on world trends down here, the average Saffer oke still thinks dangling his arm out the car window with a Marlboro between his fingers, like a baboon's tail hanging from its ring-piece, looks pretty cool bru, and sends out a lekker vibe to any chicks who might check him on the road. Never mind the raging inferno he starts when he lets his cigarette butt fly on a hot summer's day or the general stompie-landscape litter he's contributing to otherwise. The filthy-fingered philistine. Remember, philistine: deep down you know that everyone hates you. (See **Litterers**, *Kak 1*.)

Stupid advertising

"How many ways can you communicate?" asks one of those very loud HTC ads. Then it lists the ways:

1. SMS
2. MMS

3. Instant messaging
4. Social networking
5. Email
6. Phone call
7. Office mobile

Then it says, "The options are infinite."

The options are not infinite, HTC. There are seven options. Seven. Not infinite. Stop being stupid.

Super Signs

Mine dumps, check. Pollution haze, check. Lack of ameliorating geographical features, check. Hideous architecture all over the place, check. Let's see, how can we make Joburg even uglier? Ah! Super Signs! Otherwise known as very big billboards. We'll combine massive eyesores with tremendously invasive advertising that ruins what's left of the view and increases public marketing exposure even more.

Super Signs: not super.

The Sunday liquor ban

The greatest civil-rights atrocity of the apartheid era – aside from the censorship of all pornography, of course – was the God-fearing government's decree that liquor could not be sold on a Sunday. Indeed, there is no denying what a depraved, inhuman lot those Nats were. Thank the Lord for Nelson Mandela and the separation of church and state.

Today we are blessed with a modern forward-thinking country that allows star-free breasts in magazines, as well as – not to be sniffed at – the public co-mingling of people of different skin colours. But oddly, even though you can order a beer in a restaurant on any day of the week, you still can't buy a bottle of wine from Pick n Pay on a Sunday. Which can be a great inconvenience if you're in the mood for an end-of-weekend binge-drinking session.

It's time Jesus intervened and put things right.

Terms and conditions
HERE'S AN AWESOME OFFER!

With lots of sucky terms and conditions in really small writing that would have you running for the hills if you could actually be bothered to read them. But you can't. So they molest you. For example, if there's a free set of air tickets up for grabs on your next cellphone upgrade, you'll most likely find out while signing the contract that you have a window period of approximately 90 seconds in which to use them. Not that it matters because there won't be any seats available anyway.

Run for the hills while you still have your dignity.

"They"

As in "they broke into my house", "they stole my car" and "they are ruining the country". It's such a commonly used euphemism – most frequently employed by bitter expats and when-we Saffers who voted "No" in 1992 – that most of us don't think twice about it. We should.

Firstly, "they" is plural. So if it was only one guy, well, maybe it was "he"… And secondly, it implies there is a special group of people, known to everyone, responsible for all the terrible things that happen in this country. Not to racially obsess or anything (see **Racial obsessing**, *Kak 1*), but this is simply a disguised form of racial obsessing. Might as well just say "the masses" or "those bloody blacks" – which is what "they" were known as a couple of decades ago.

"To end this call press hash or hang up"

Why must I be told how to end a telephone call? Did I think this was a very special telephone call that required a complicated code to end it? Or are you trying to fleece a few extra cents out of me by keeping me on the line for an extra two seconds? A million times over and you've got some extra profit, hey?

If you treat people like simpletons, I guess they'll end up behaving like simpletons.

The Tour de France

There's something inherently unsatisfactory about watching a bunch of skinny spandex monkeys with oversized calves pedaling their cheating arses up and down mountains for three weeks. Maybe EPO and testosterone just aren't my recreational drugs of choice. Guess I'm more a crack-cocaine kinda guy.

Tow-truck drivers

Opportunistic low-profile vultures, lurking at the kerbside and willing disaster upon you and your fellow road users – then screaming through the streets at highly illegal speeds, putting to shame all minibus-taxi drivers in the vicinity and exponentially increasing the possibility of yet another crash occurring, to throw a winch around a busted-up car while the driver lies in a pool of his own blood wondering when the paramedics are going to arrive. The definitive low-life scum of the universe.

Traffic circles

In other parts of the world it's called a roundabout, and it facilitates traffic flow as drivers yield to the right and indicate correctly when entering and exiting. Here it's called a traffic circle and it's a licence for complete pandemonium. Minibus taxis and BMWs just drive, student chicks in Opel Corsas think it's a four-way stop, SUV kugels on their cellphones don't have the first fucking clue what's going on, and everyone else just hopes for the best. Then there's the two-lane traffic circle, and that's a licence for complete *and utter* pandemonium…

Traffic cops

Look, I hate you guys even when you're just doing your job, but when you sit lurking in suburbia waiting to catch me doing 68km/h in a 60 zone when you could be apprehending the multiple-violations minibus driver ferrying 27 people along Main Road in an unlicensed, unroadworthy deathtrap, then that makes me hate you even more.* And then I top up on the loathing when I have to negotiate my way through yet another lights-out intersection and you're nowhere to be seen, unless it's around the corner soliciting bribes from soccer moms jumping stop streets. And what's the deal with parking tickets that are invariably more than a pensioner's monthly payout? What if I'm a pensioner and I get a ticket? Sometimes there's just nowhere to park, you know? And if there is, it's "guarded" by some palooka hassling me for money, even if I'm just dropping off a DVD or picking up a coffee.

I don't know why I even bother leaving the house any more.

* And even more when I recall the stat that there are nearly a million unlicensed, unroadworthy cars on our roads – nearly one in ten – contributing greatly to our R50 billion annual road carnage. R50 billion! That's one-and-a-half arms deals!

Trucks on single-lane highways

Could be doing 140km/h, but no, it's 65 and increasingly creative volleys of extended swearing behind Sarel Potgieter's 24-wheeler hauling sheep off to the abattoir. Check your mirrors, Sarel. There are a dozen cars behind you and we'd greatly appreciate it if you pulled over. Or your truck spontaneously exploded.

Morgan Tsvangirai

Something tells me he's not the next Gandhi.

Two-prong plugs

There are times when you get that feeling that human development is actually going backwards. While we think we're forging ahead in a technological blaze of glory, sometimes it's hard not to believe we're just fooling ourselves. Take the two-prong plug. Invented in the 1920s, this is a piece of technology that, logic must conclude, has got worse over time. Anyone who came up with a plug that continually falls out of its socket would be a laughing stock, hence we must deduce that it didn't used to do this. But now, after many decades of massive electrical-appliances roll-outs – toasters and blenders and vibrators and whatnot, all launched with great fanfare and wonder – you're lucky if you can angle grind just one angle without the plug popping out of the adaptor. Or get ten minute's recharging before your giant half-kilogram cellphone charger falls off the wall. Or blow-dry your hair and move the dryer at the same time. (Not that I blow-dry my hair, but, you know, the women have a point here.)

Interestingly not all two-prong plugs are bad. To try to work out what's going on here you need to realise that there are now no less than 13 different styles of plugs worldwide, the result of various stubborn countries wanting to do things their way instead of just adopting the US standard. That's what nationalism gets you: a couple of world wars and 13 different plugs. Unfortunately, South Africa ended up with a particularly sucky plug that requires adaptors for every second appliance – and then we ended up with a sucky two-prong plug as our alternative.

Just so you know who to direct your frustration at the next time your charger falls off the wall, the two-prong plug used in South Africa is the French type. *Morceau de merde!*

U

Umshini Wami

My my, was our man with a plan Jacob Zuma upset when the xenophobic mobs that ran riot in 2008 took to singing *Umshini Wami* while brutalising and murdering foreigners. Upset and, apparently, surprised. Which would make him the only person alive who could not have predicted the possibility of a song about machine guns being used as an accompaniment to violent crime in a country beset with violent crime.

Looking to the future, JZ, here are some songs to avoid popularising among your supporters, whether in public appearances or as a ring tone:

Hit Em Up by Tupac*
Bombtrack by Rage Against The Machine
Bullet In The Head by Rage Against The Machine**
Sound Of A Gun by Audioslave
Kill For The Country by Springbok Nude Girls
Nonstop Violence by Apoptygma Berzerk
I Want Your Sex by George Michael

* This song is about fetching "your Glock". Don't be tempted, JZ!

** Probably a good idea to stay away from Rage Against The Machine altogether.

Unceasing self-help books

If it's not Rhonda Byrne telling us the secret (it's not really a secret after that, Rhonda…), or Eckhart Tolle awakening our potentials (yawn), or Anthony Robbins encouraging us to release the power within or introducing us to personal power or informing us about our unlimited power (I'm picking up on a power theme here), then it's some other greasy snake-oil salesman you've never heard of revealing this month's cure for your every woe. They just don't stop, and the South African top-ten bestseller list, by rule, includes three or four of the bastards.

Here's bald-headed Robin Sharma, also known as The Monk Who Sold His Ferrari, which is meant to sound impressive and humbling. But who buys a Ferrari in the first place? A self-obsessed twat, that's who. And who sells his Ferrari and then tells everyone how liberating it is? A self-righteous twat, I'm guessing. Now if his next book was *The Monk Who Bought An Aston Martin*, then perhaps I'd listen. It isn't, though. It's *The Greatness Guide*. Which is, at the very least, rather presumptuous.

But it doesn't look nearly as bad as *Your Best Life Now: 7 Steps To Living At Your Full Potential* by Joel Osteen. Have you seen Joel Osteen? Well, if you haven't, there's a great big picture of him on the cover. You can't miss it. He looks like a cheese-eating douche bag. My best life now would in no way include reading *Your Best Life Now*. Rather it would involve stringing up Joel Osteen by his feet and inserting ever-increasing amounts of wasabi down his nose. And burning all the quick-buck "publishing phenomenon" self-help books out there. Well, maybe not my best life, but certainly my most satisfying life. (See **Self-help programmes**, *Kak 1*.)

Underground parking

Expensive!

Unnecessary talking objects

Talking lifts are the new thing. "Going up" and "going down", I understand, but you'd think that blind people, with their well developed sense of hearing, don't need an annoying voice that gets exponentially more annoying every time you hear it (which is a lot when you're staying in a hotel for a few days, believe me) to tell them when the doors are opening? There's the sound of the doors opening for that. Surely?

And urinal-ad loudspeakers? There you are at Cinema Nouveau trying to take a whizz while simultaneously trying to avoid accidentally looking at other men's manacondas, and suddenly the advertisement in front of you is talking. The print ad is always welcome: it gives you a point of focus and lets you pass the time if you've got a bit of stage fright, but when it starts talking that's just taking multitasking one step too far. See and pee at the same time, maybe. See, pee and listen… that's just asking too much. (See **Drivers yakking on their cellphones.**)

Useless made-in-China toys

A hundred flowers bloom, a hundred schools of thought contend. Glorious republic of scientific development and harmonious society led by honourable great leader and purveyor of cheap shit toys to kids humbly requests anyone who has ever had their children's Christmas present survive past January to contact the Honourable Co-operative for People's Goods in Zhejiang Province urgently and let them know of this terrible mistake. They will immediately execute the traitor who allowed this violation of Chinese manufacturing standards to occur.

Once a communist stronghold, China is fast becoming the next big world superpower on the back of an unprecedented industrialisation movement and the seemingly inherent ability not to give the faintest fart about production values. If there is a way to do something, China will work out how to do it quicker, cheaper, worse and far, far unhealthier. In a sense, this is what true capitalism is all about: maximising profits, buggering everything else. And Chinese toy making is the perfect microcosm of this attitude.

Here's a Thomas & Friends train, kids. It's covered in various hazardous materials, including lead. Lead causes brain damage. Can you say brain damage?

And here are some toys in Vladivostok that contain phenol and formaldehyde. Who can tell me what phenol is known for? Yes, the Nazis used it in their euthanasia programmes. Very good! And you might recognise formaldehyde as an important embalming ingredient.

And this is an Aqua Dot, the Australian Toy Association's toy of the year for 2007, which has sent children in the US and Australia into non-responsive comas. It is coated in a chemical that when ingested turns into the date-rape drug gamma-hydroxybutyrate (GHB). Who can spell gamma-hydroxybutyrate for me?

Damn, if the Chinese can't even be bothered with basic health standards, to the point that millions of toys have to be recalled at a time from around the world, I guess we shouldn't be too shocked when little Barry's new red toy tractor instantaneously turns pink on exposure to sunlight before the wheels fall off. I think it's time they made a film on the topic. One of those pioneering Hollywood movies that opens viewers' eyes to a very real contemporary issue, just like *I Now Pronounce You Chuck And Larry* showed everyone that being nasty to gays is not very nice. Arnold Schwarzenegger could play a defective GI Joe soldier that comes to life in a remake of *Total Recall*. They'd have to translate it into Mandarin, though, otherwise it would be a bit pointless. I see it now: *Total Lecall: Levenge Of The Stlychnine-Coated Wallior*. It's got brockbuster written all over it.

V

Valentine's day

The birds are atwitter, the flowers are in bloom and romance fills the air... So obviously it isn't Valentine's Day, then, that day of commercial coercion, when Hallmark tries to guilt you into buying cards and balloons, and Gerald your flower guy, who on any other day of the year is just a decent guy trying to make a living, takes it upon himself to charge R40 for a fast-withering rose. Fuck you, Gerald.

Time for a DVD marathon, sweetheart. Either *Terminators* I through III, or maybe *The Hunt For Red October*, *Crimson Tide* and *Das Boot*.

"Variant spelling" plans

There is an Englishman, one Ken Smith, who believes that certain frequently misspelt words should be accepted into the English language as "variant spellings". A criminology lecturer at Bucks New University in Buckinghamshire, Mr Smith observes – in the *Times Higher Education Supplement*, no less – that he finds himself correcting the same student spelling mistakes year after year: arguement instead of argument, twelth for twelfth, truely for truly, Febuary for February and so on. In the same way that knowledgeable can be spelt with or without the second "e", his logic dictates, a selection of the most commonly confused words should also be allowed to be spelt in different ways. A professor John Wells of University College London wants to take things one step further: he thinks any modern-day spelling is fine: u or you, ur or your, copy or coppy, salad or sallad and the like.

On the face of it, these are silly ideas. You don't have to be a neurotic grammar nerd who proofreads Chinese-takeaway menus to realise this. As such, it would be tempting simply to suggest to Mr Smith and Mr Wells that their arguements are truely poor and they best be on their way.

But perhaps you do need to be a neurotic grammar nerd to realise just how ominous these proposals of Mr Smith and Mr Wells really are. Luckily, there is such a nerd at hand... and let me start by saying this: Jebus Chris! Are they cretans?

It's not like the human race isn't on the precipice already. As we stand today, the world is inundated with text-speak, forum abbreviations, general retarded spellings and smiley faces (see *Kak 1* for all of these), without giving licence to the unwashed morons out there to spell however they want and damn the consequences. The very thought is enough to crush your soul. But it's not just the resulting grammatical free-for-all that will follow as surely as night follows day (oh, apostrophe, how I despair for your bleak future!); on the contrary, there are greater issues at stake. Discipline, patience, care, understanding, self-control, respect, love, basic human intelligence. When spelling is abandoned then so too is our very civilisation.

Yes, Mr Smith – if that is your real name – and Mr Wells – whomever or whatever you may be – your ideas, far from being simple time-savers, are actually requests to shake the very foundations on which modern existence is built. The fate of the world hangs in the balance here. If we can't get this right then there is no hope. We may as well just send up the nukes right now.

Zwelinzima Vavi

Here is the apparent order of events when Cosatu general secretary Zwelinzima Vavi has something to say:

1. Open mouth.
2. Talk.
3. Think. (Optional.)

There is in fact a school of thought that Zwelinzima Vavi is not actually talking when he opens his mouth but that a miniature microphone, invisible to the naked eye, is simply rattling off a selection of pre-recorded sound bytes to endorse Jacob Zuma and/or Cosatu and to create a generally bothersome atmosphere so as to ensure he is rewarded with the position of minister of labour in the near future.

Hmmm, sounds plausible to me. As such, here is how I imagine a conversation between Vavi and me might go:

ME: Hello, Mr V-

VAVI: Comrades, we must follow the mighty Zuma!

ME: I beg your pardon, I ju-

VAVI: We must forge ahead with the revolution!

ME: Why do you keep going on about the revo-

VAVI: We must zero-rate basic food stuffs!

ME: But they are-

VAVI: We must ignore this Nazi propaganda!

ME: What the f-

VAVI: Kill does not necessarily mean kill!

ME: Would you like a tranquiliser of some sort?

VAVI: I like using words like "so-called" and "mischievous" and "kill"!

ME: Relaxing herbal tea?

VAVI: I won't apologise for anything!

ME: Warm mug of shut the fuck up?

Verbing

Take a noun, such as the noun "verb", and then just magically verb it into a verb and – presto! – you've got "verbing". Honestly, it's not that tricky. There's eventing, gifting, guesting, tasking, actioning, architecting, dialoguing, favouriting, suiciding…

Can you "physical" someone? Probably not, but apparently you can "out-physicalise" someone. That is according to ex-tennis pro Greg Rusedski, who is, amazingly, not American. But he was born in Canada, so close enough.

People who make up words like this should be known as assholiosillyflaps because verbing is stupid and it dumbs language.

Vida e Caffé service

The whole shouting, vibrant cool-bra thing was different and hip for a while, sure, I'll give you that. But it's loud and annoying now, and sometimes I just want to read the newspaper in peace. Time to get a new angle, guys.

Coffee's still decent though.

Violence as a kneejerk reaction

"Jis ou perd, die geweld in die land is heeltemal te erg…
"Excuse me…"
"Ek kan nie glo hoe poes-min daar aan gedoen word nie!"
"Um, sorry, can I get past please?"
"Soek jy 'n klap, soutie?"
"Er, no. I was just hoping to make my way to the bar area."
"Ek sal jou moer!"
"Right… Perhaps I'll just back off and let you continue drinking your brandy and coke in peace, shall I?"

Is this guy a fokken doos or what?

Now, let's be clear on something: not all Afrikaners live up to the "Dutchman" reputation as aggro troublemakers. Not by a long shot. But we've all come across those who make violence and threats of violence a first resort in all they do as a guiding principle with which to run their lives. These are the guys who go out clubbing with the express intention of getting into a fight; who wander their neighbourhoods at night looking for bergies to donner; who shoot their wives for stealing the blankets; who end up turning into Eugene de Kock given the opportunity.

But you don't have to be Afrikaans to behave this way. Just bump into a Kempton Park breeker's "dolly" to find this out. And you don't have to be white either. The Zulu man, for example, has been known to lay down a good beating, be it on his wife or the local foreigner. In fact, as evidenced by our murder and mayhem, most South African ethnic groups seem to include high percentages of people whose kneejerk reaction is to raise a fist or a gun rather than engage their brains and debate a problem when one arises. Recent stabbing-inundated ANC meetings spring to mind.

The rest of South Africa could learn a lot from us passive-aggressive WASPs who, when put out, take comfort from bottling up our rage into a secret supply of ulcer-generating fury, which later manifests itself in the psychological tormenting of our children and people over whom we may have marginal influence. Sometimes we write books.

Vodafone mobile internet
"While attempting to connect, an error with the number 619 occurred. – The port is disconnected."

Error 31, 618 and 678 are other common excuses for having to restart your laptop every second time you try to connect. (And it is literally *every second time*. As with the *FHM* exclamation marks, I'm not exaggerating here.) By my logic, that means there are at least 678 potential errors that can occur. And that tells you something right there.

The anger is enormous, by the way. Enormous.

Louis Vuitton

Over-priced crap designed for Asian cross-dressers. Except the ties. They're nice.

"Warmest personal regards"

That's just next level. (See **"Warm regards"**, *Kak 1*.)

Water-saving shower heads

Yes, they're environmentally friendly but that doesn't mean they don't suck. Especially when the dams are at 110 per cent capacity and the Cape winter is raging outside your window, dropping sheets of water to the ground as you cower under a miserable dribble like you're being weed on by an old man with a prostate the size of a grapefruit. I'm all for hugging a tree and conserving water (I mean, I *never* do dishes), but when it comes to showering, I want a monsoon on my head with water droplets the size of squash balls. It's a life luxury that we all deserve.

Luke Watson's walking style

Like he's got invisible watermelons under his arms. What's that all about?

Wickable apparel as casual wear

In case you haven't heard, you've got absolutely no chance of success when attempting any sort of athletic feat unless you're wearing a wickable garment of some kind. This has been proven by scientific research.

Want to run a half marathon? Sorry, you're not going to make it – unless your vest is wickable. Gonna climb Kilimanjaro? You'll be needing a new wickable T-shirt every day, then. Don't even *think* of wearing a normal cotton T-shirt. Are you mental? The sweat! How can you even put one foot in front of the other if you can't regulate the moisture on your skin? You may very well die on the first day.

Did you know that Edmund Hillary's first words on summitting Mount Everest in 1953 were, "Thank god for my wickable jockstrap!"? Oh wait, no they weren't. But if he were still alive I bet he'd loudly declare "I love my wickable jockstrap!" every morning as he got out of bed. Actually, no I don't bet that. I bet he'd tell wannabe adventure nuts obsessed with "outdoor apparel" to stop being such marketing suckers and harden the fuck up.

It's got so bad now that some of them see fit to wear it when they're walking in the street. Or going to the cinema. This way, everyone else walking in the street or going to the cinema can see that they clearly partake in regular bouts of strenuous outdoor exercise and are therefore cool. The thing that they seem to forget is that wickable material is very shiny. A bit like polyester. Which it usually is. So not only have they fallen for the outdoor-apparel marketing scam when they'd get better value by just shaving their legs (god forbid), but they look like walking ballbags. And they've turned themselves into human fire hazards.

"Sorry, buddy, I accidentally set fire to your highly flammable shiny kit. It looks awesome with flames leaping off it."

"Aarrghhh! The burning! The burning!"

"What's that, boychee? Can't hear you properly. You seem a bit excited and aren't enunciating your words very clearly. Say, never seen you run that fast before…"

As with many of today's woes, you can safely blame the rise of wickable clothing as casual wear on cyclists. When climates change and the earth finally stops rotating on its axis, it'll be the cyclists' fault.

"Withheld caller"

Look, I'm a naturally suspicious guy. So if I see "Withheld caller" when my phone rings I'm just going to assume you're a tele-salesman. Or SARS. Either way, I'm not answering.

What's with trying to conceal who you are anyway? You wouldn't ring my doorbell wearing a balaclava, would you? Well, not unless you were trying to take something from me. Which is why I think you're a tele-salesman. Or SARS.

The woeful movie choices of Nicolas Cage

When you think Nicolas Cage you probably don't think Hollywood freak-show jackass (see **Tom Cruise**). But take a closer look at the never-ending procession of egregious American pap he's starred in since the late '90s and you've got to wonder. Either the man rang up a scary mafia-related debt a while back and he's till paying it off, or he suddenly stopped looking at scripts, perhaps as the result of an unusual brain disease that has left him with a mullet hairstyle in place of the ability to read.

The watershed mark in Nicolas Cage's career is, of course, *Face/Off*, a giant pile of cinematic crapiola if ever there was one (see **Hollywood special-effects self-indulgence, Kak 1**). Before the release of that John Woo explosive-slo-mo wankathon, his film résumé was pretty solid: *Raising Arizona*, *Wild At Heart*, *Kiss Of Death*, *Leaving Las Vegas*, among others. Since then, though, he's been pimping himself out to the highest bidders, as long as they're willing to film the same one-dimensional character with the same pained expression running from, to or through explosions. Preferably with a bored, deadpan voice-over at some point.

The comprehension of Cage's decline comes with the realisation that he has starred in at least ten of the 50 worst big-budget movies of all time in a little over a decade, viz:

1997 *Face/Off*
1998 *City Of Angels*
2000 *Gone In 60 Seconds*
2001 *Captain Corelli's Mandolin*
2002 *Windtalkers*
2004 *National Treasure*
2006 *World Trade Center*
2007 *Ghost Rider* and *National Treasure: Book Of Secrets*
2008 *Bangkok Dangerous*

So what do you think? Gambling debts? Hooker addiction? Or rare brain disease?

Woolworths food stores

Woolworths doesn't just stock food on its shelves; oh no, gentle shopper, it offers a wide range of aggravations, annoyances and inconveniences to pop into your basket too – and unlike the various food products that are so very often out of stock, these will always be in supply.

Let's start at the plastic-wrapped-vegetable end of the store, where you can purchase a three-pack of garlic, but not a one-pack of garlic. Trivial perhaps, and yet it causes great pain: an I-just-ate-too-much-garlic-and-will-wake-up-with-a-dry-mouth-tonight indigestion kind of pain. I don't need three garlics! Unless perhaps I'm shopping for a family of ten Frenchmen. In which case I'll save on overweight-baggage charges and do it in France. The Third World could be awash with nutritious, AIDS-defeating garlic if it wasn't for the wasteful Woolworths three-pack – which is, I'd suggest, a bank-fee-reminiscent way of making us spend R10 on garlic instead of R3. Scumbags.

Then there's the "perfectly ripe" fruit, which a) is wrapped in enough plastic to make a mockery of all the proudly displayed organic hoo-ha that lines the walls and b) is either a relative term, in that the plums I've just eaten are perfectly ripe when compared to my wastepaper basket, or a hit-and-miss hope-no-one-complains marketing tool.

And on that note, whatever has happened to the so-called quality of produce that Woolworths has always lorded as its reason for existence? There was a time when you could suffer the budget-draining prices because the food was just so good, but it's beginning to piss me off now. To be fair, it's often still good these days, but it's often equally bad. Food-poisoning-inducing wraps, rank chicken, appalling bread, chicken-and-noodle soup that looks like thrush in a bowl... all cutting close to the bone here, Woolies.

Of course, the prices are the real kicker. Particularly the little extras that they leave lying tantalisingly in your path. Mmm, biltong... At R75.95 for a piddly 180g bag. It's dried meat, damn it! Do the maths and that's over R420 a kilo. Which translates into a moerse rip-off.

And still I go back time and again. Better than shopping at Melissa's, I suppose. (See **Overpriced deli food that's nothing more than glorified Woolworths.**)

X

Once upon a time an "x" at the end of a letter symbolised a passionate or, at least, flirty kiss. Now, at the end of an email or SMS it represents a hackneyed meaningless sign-off, kind of like a cross between those ultimate abominations of modern communication, "lol" and smiley faces (see **"Lol"** and **Smiley faces**, *Kak 1*). And yet *everyone* uses them. Relatives, work associates, casual acquaintances. Even Jamie Oliver who, never one to hold back, is partial to signing off his letters to magazine readers with a triple xxx.

Look, I don't want kisses from you unless you're my girlfriend. Or maybe Kate Beckinsale. So don't go signing off your written correspondence with me with an x unless you're my girlfriend or Kate Beckinsale. Okay? Oliver, back the hell off.

Xenon headlights

They're so frikking clever that they can invent headlights to map the road and look around corners, but they can't design the damn things to not burn out my retina every time a BMW 650 comes speeding up my arse. Who buys a 650 anyway?

Y

Yebo djembe drums

Vodacom. So brand aware, so market savvy, so hip. One of South Africa's favourite companies in fact. Which kind of defies belief, really, when you think that it gave us that effing meerkat (see **The Vodacom meerkat, *Kak 1*)***. Clearly we're a forgiving bunch. But the Vodacom honchos are pushing their luck with the Yebo djembe drums…

In case you're not the sporting type, Yebo djembe drums are the little plastic drum things, all nicely bedecked in Vodacom colours, that get issued to virtually every spectator at certain high-profile sports matches. Literally, they dish them out by the tens of thousands. During the game they're not so bad because they entertain people with limited attention spans who've forgotten there's a game of rugby on, and they help drown out the sound of offensive spectators (see **Booing fans**). It's afterwards that the pain comes. In the streets. When *everyone* with a djembe drum becomes an offensive spectator. And when you realise that some Vodacom marketing über-geek probably got a half-million-rand bonus for coming up with an invention that rivals the vuvuzela (see **Vuvuzelas, *Kak 1*)** for aggravation overload.

* Which, word has it, has finally been scrapped. Sweet mercies. Special thanks to DraftFCB, Vodacom's ad agency, for creating that droopy-eyed little bastard. Amazingly, these guys also came up with the brilliant "We've been having it" campaign – which Vodacom, in its wisdom, decided to can after two months. Just when we thought they'd redeemed themselves...

Z

Zeffed-out Crocs

Evidently, and much to our disappointment, the entire world did not read the original *Kak*, otherwise the current global fashion catastrophe taking place may well have been avoided. (See **Crocs**, *Kak 1*.) Not only are Crocs still around but there is now an entire range of Croc-based footwear, including Croc pumps, Croc slippers, fur-lined Crocs and the like, as well as horrendous Croc accessories. There is also an official website and, at the V&A Waterfront, a dedicated Crocs shop. I've walked past it (though an invisible force field prevented me from entering): it is hideous squared, a microcosm of hell. And the situation reached crisis point recently, when the South African Olympic team wore matching Crocs at the 2008 opening ceremony. Something must be done.

Variant spelling and zeffed-out Crocs – I'm telling you, the future of humanity rests with these two issues. (See **"Variant spelling"** plans.)

Zuma as a Christian name

In August 2008, Gwen Stefani gave birth to her second child and named it Zuma. Has the entire world gone absolutely befok in the head?

ALSO BY TWO DOGS...

Is It Just Me Or Is Everything Kak?
By Tim Richman
and Grant Schreiber
The original *Kak* is a funny, acerbic and deeply satirical A-to-Z frothy that earned best-seller status in South Africa, as well as widespread critical praise. Car guards, bank fees, quotas, Hansie Cronjé, Manto Tshabalala-Msimang, Telkom, Eskom, the Vodacom meerkat, Paris Hilton's parents, Jacob Zuma and more all faced the music...

"Quite splendidly takes the piss out of South Africa" – *Sunday Times*

ISBN 978 192013 720 5

Is Dit Net Ek Of Is Als Tos?
Deur Chopper Charlie & Griffin
Die Afrikaanse weergawe van die blitsverkoper *Is It Just Me Or Is Everything Kak?* wat kla oor allerlei goed wat gewone Suid-Afrikaners 'n akute pyn in die agterstewe gee. Alhoewel die Afrikaanse titel losweg gebaseer is op die Engelse weergawe is die onderwerpe, humor en styl doelbewus aangepas vir die Afrikaanse leser. Meer as 150 aspekte van vandag se lewe loop kwaai deur insluitende die AWB, Blou Bul ondersteuners, call centres, Eskom, Oppikoppi boneheads, Saffas, Telkom, Joost van der Westhuizen, Vereeniging...

ISBN 978 192013 717 5

See www.twodogs.co.za for more on these and other books